W9-ARD-634

MOSES HESS

UTOPIAN SOCIALIST

by John Weiss

DETROIT   WAYNE STATE UNIVERSITY PRESS   1960

SOCIAL SCIENCES

WAYNE STATE UNIVERSITY STUDIES   Number 8

Library cf Congress Catalog Card Number

Copyright © 1960, All rights reserved

Wayne State University Press, Detroit 2, Michigan

92
H586w

To

Mabel Weiss Hollander

RANGER JUNIOR COLLEGE LIBRARY

11360

Preface

All those who have been interested in Moses Hess owe an immense debt to the thorough, painstaking, and excellent scholarship of Edmund Silberner of the University of Jerusalem. I have depended heavily on his research, and all who are interested in the history of socialism will be pleased to know that Mr. Silberner is at present working on a biography of Moses Hess which will certainly become the standard biographical source. I must also thank Helmut Hirsch of Roosevelt University who so graciously consented to allow me to inspect some of his work on Moses Hess. Whatever clarity and felicity the reader finds in the writing is the result of the excellent training I received at Columbia University in the Seminar of Jacques Barzun. Those who are acquainted with Mr. Barzun's brilliant work, *Darwin, Marx, Wagner: Critique of a Heritage,* will see that I have followed his general interpretation of the nature and value of utopian socialism.

J.W.

Contents

Introduction

A simple count of the varieties of socialist ideas produced and propagated during the first half of the nineteenth century will show that this was the most creative period in the history of socialist theory. These were the fruitful years of Saint-Simon, Fourier, Fichte, Owen, Sismondi, Godwin, Weitling, and Proudhon, as well as a host of lesser figures. Indeed, it would be difficult to find any general and important socialist idea or ideal not known or presented by some of these men. New ideas have often been modifications of general principles familiar to the utopian Socialists of the first half of the nineteenth century—modifications usually made in the light of economic principles and facts unknowable then.

Nevertheless, the greatest change in the history of socialist theory has usually been dated from the middle of the nineteenth century. The use of the catchwords *utopian* and *scientific* to denote that change, however, indicates that it was caused not so much by the introduction of new ideas as by the popularity of a new attitude. To be "scientific" rather than utopian meant, among other differences, to be tough and "realistic," and, specifically, to refuse to be taken in by naive illusions about the goodness of man and his amenability to moral persuasion. One index of the popularity of such "realism" is to be found in the writing of the history of socialist theory itself. Too often the rich variety of early nineteenth century socialism has been sacrificed, and utopian socialism used merely to demonstrate the superiority of "realistic" moral toughness, as well as the pre-eminence of the man most responsible for the new attitude, Karl Marx.

So it is that until recently most of the early Socialists have been regarded as important only if, by some happy accident, they can be shown to have prepared the way for the great system of the alleged master of them all. We are left with the impression that we are dealing either with hazy-minded and fumbling "precursors," or foolish, dreaming "Utopians," "non-scientific" (what greater insult nowadays?) to the core. Still, I believe—as others have suggested—that Marx's influence resulted not so much from his originality as from the way in which, by purging socialism of what he considered an excess of moral idealism, he was able to construct out of ideas not unknown before his time, a system supremely capable of appealing to a generation distrusting and despising romanticism, and entertaining some crude and simple notions about science and reality.[1] By this I do not mean to deny Marx's genius; he remains the most important and influential Socialist of the nineteenth century. I think it important to note, however, that his astounding influence was not simply the result of his being right where others were wrong, but was in great part caused by his single minded appeal to the "scientific" prejudices of an era.[2]

Among the evidences of Marx's influence, not the least is this: of the many German Socialists of the thirties and forties of the last century, only Moses Hess and Karl Rodbertus are familiar names to most students of socialism; and they are familiar mainly because Rodbertus announced the theory of surplus value before Marx, and Hess introduced Marx and Engels to the literature of socialism. It is doubtful if Hess would be known at all had he not managed to praise Marx extravagantly on different occasions, and so find for his name, at least, a place in the footnotes of most biographies of Marx. After 1848, Marx and Engels did all they could to blast what reputation Hess had, and the second part of the *Communist Manifesto* contains an unfair denunciation of German "true socialism," by which Marx and Engels meant the socialism of Moses Hess—then known as the "father of German socialism." [3] As for Rodbertus, Engels did his best in later years to disprove his priority over the master.[4]

If we are to understand German utopian socialism, we can do no better than to turn to the work of Moses Hess. Of all German Socialists before Marx and Engels, Hess was the most influential among his contemporaries and was, in fact, the chief theorist of a small group who called themselves the "True Socialists." Like most of the radicals of the day, his political idealism was stimulated by the tremendous transformation caused by the French and Industrial Revolutions, and Hess shared in that great awareness of new possibilities brought forth by those years of dramatic political and economic change. Hess's works are dominated by that same hopeful and enthusiastic idealism which marked the Forty-eighters as they contemplated the seemingly unlimited opportunities for the reform of politics and society. It is no accident that socialist literature should have had its golden age during the years from 1789 to 1848, and that German socialism in particular should enter its first creative period during the height of the Romantic era in Germany—the eighteen-forties. These were the years later to be known as the *Vormaerz*, a term chosen to suggest their unity as a time of widespread idealism and to indicate that they formed a prelude to the revolutionary enthusiasm of the days of March, 1848.

Like Karl Marx and most of the first German Socialists, Hess drew from the same two sources of inspiration: French utopian socialism and German philosophical idealism. Paris was Hess's second home in the eighteen-forties, when the ideas of Saint-Simon, Fourier, Proudhon, Blanc, and Cabet were discussed in pamphlets and journals, argued on street corners, and preached from the lecture platform. Indeed, there is no better example of how men in one country are able to draw lessons from the experience of another than that given by the history of the beginnings of German socialism. Until 1848, French utopian socialism *was*, to the Germans, socialism. And in agreement with the French Socialists, Hess stressed the necessity of class cooperation, the need to avoid revolution, and the powerful influence of ideas and ethics in history. Throughout his life Hess greatly admired the work of those who had first introduced him to socialism and had taught him that the best weapons in the struggle for social reform were those of moral persuasion and education.

Hess's activities on behalf of radical social reform, however, did not end with the eighteen-forties; he continued to publish, organize, and agitate until his death in 1875. The last half of his career was partly spent in an attempt to counteract the rejection of the utopian attitude consequent upon the increasing popularity of "scientific" socialism. The fifties and sixties were, of course, the years of transition from utopian to "scientific" socialism; increasingly during those years Socialists tended to believe in the necessity of class struggle, the certainty of bloody revolution, the dependence of ideas on powerful economic "forces," and the inefficacy of mere moral appeals. Marxism may not have become popular until the last two decades of the century, but during the fifties and sixties—and often without the aid of Marx—German Socialists began to reject the utopian tradition. How true this is we will see when we come to Hess's work during the eighteen fifties, for then Hess, like Marx, found it necessary to deny his own utopian past. Unlike Marx, however, Hess in the last twenty years of his life found the means to reaffirm his utopianism.

I have said that Hess was strongly influenced by the utopian attitude he found in the French Socialists. Important as this influence was, however, the influence of German philosophical idealism was even more fundamental. The work of Hegel, and especially of Fichte—the first German utopian Socialist—took precedence in time and importance over the work of Saint-Simon and Fourier. (This is true even though Hess, in his first work, called himself a "disciple of Spinoza"; for, as we shall see, Hess treated Spinoza's pantheism as if it were the final synthesis of the principles of the great trinity of German philosophy—Kant, Fichte, and Hegel.) From German philosophy Hess learned that history is a vast struggle between unlimited spirit and obdurate matter, with spirit destined to be the ultimate victor. Hess was not a philosopher by profession; but it was not necessary to be a philosopher in the eighteen-forties in order to be aware of the precepts of German idealism, for then it was *the* philosophy. From the pulpit, in the lecture hall, and among the bohemians in the *Bierstube*, German students heard again and again of the march of the Absolute Spirit through world history. Before his trips to Paris, before he had been any more than vaguely aware of socialism, Hess had become convinced that the perfect society was to be the final and complete realization of the Absolute Spirit in history, and the embodiment of the Moral Idea on earth. Under the influence of German idealism, then, Hess became a Utopian before he became a utopian Socialist.

Correspondingly, Hess did not find it necessary to turn Hegel "right-side up." And although Hess used the dialectical method, he was not a dialectical materialist but, true to the lessons of Fichte and Hegel, was a dialectical Idealist. This is to say that for Hess the decisive forces in history were ideas and ethics, and not, as for the Marxists, the development of the means of production and the consequent class struggle. For Hess, the dialectical struggle was a struggle between man's increasing moral awareness and his social environment, and not, again as with the Marxists, between opposed economic forces, with ideas tagging along behind, largely determined by class relationships, and exerting hardly more than the force of inertia. Following the German Idealists, Hess saw history as the story of the gradual surrender of the forces of nature and the brute materials of civilization to the knowledge and will of men. Hess readily accepted the utopian Socialists' assumption of the universal appeal of ethical claims, because he agreed with Fichte that ethics was autonomous, and not merely the reflection of immediate class interest. Hess expected that sooner or later all men, regardless of class, would accept socialism, simply because only socialism could fulfill the demands of the moral consciousness possessed by all. Hess could believe this and still be aware of the great obstacles which lay in the path of social reform because his idealism was not naive. For like Marx, Hess was aware of the "iron" laws of economics familiar to many Utopians, but unlike Marx he was convinced that man's ideals were even more forceful. Hess insisted that the so-called laws of economics which seemed to damn forever all hope of radical reform were but a delusion which would have no power as soon as man became aware that his moral nature was the mightiest force in the universe. He agreed with Fichte; the dialectic will end with the perfect society, and the final victory of the ideal over the real will be achieved by socialism. In this way, German philosophy prepared Hess to accept the existing social ideals of the French Utopians.

As we know, Marx became a Marxist by his resolve to exclude from socialism just such ideas as these. Marx's attack was part of a general change in idea and opinion which can be roughly dated from the eighteen-fifties. Science, realism, a new moral toughness—whatever one chooses to call it, and however one judges its value—assured Marx's victory over the Utopians, French and German. A large part of the appeal of Marxism lay in its attraction to a generation embittered by the outcome of the revolutions of 1848, and increasingly afraid to appear naive. It is difficult to have ideals and still not appear idealistic, and yet is not Marx's attempt to do just that mainly responsible for the brilliant intricacies of dialectical materialism? To be a Marxist was to hide one's idealism behind the pose of ruthless scientific objectivity. The day of the cynical idealist had begun, and those who would not join the march found themselves labeled as Utopians and libeled as "non-scientific." Those responsible for the victory of the political reaction in Germany helped to create an atmosphere in which such moral toughness could flourish, for indeed it was a reaction to the reaction, and the tendency to meet force with force was irresistible.

Given the political mood of Germany in the fifties, it would have been utopian to remain utopian—at least in tactics—and

Hess "reacted" right along with most German radicals. Indeed, in 1846 and 47, Hess was converted to the then established principles of "scientific" socialism by no less a figure than Karl Marx himself. After 1850 and until the rise of the brilliant Lassalle, Hess did not find his earlier moral idealism an adequate support for socialism, and he was not alone. A generation was adjusting to what seemed a new reality and by so doing were helping to bring about that new reality, as romantic idealism gave way to what has been called realism.

The utopianism of the forties, so well represented by Moses Hess, did not die out with this initial "disillusionment." In the sixties Hess aided Lassalle in bringing the utopian attitude to victories, and the influence of Lassalle's utopianism over the practice if not the theory of the Social Democratic Party of Germany was easily as great as that of the Marxists. Similarly, and even during the high tide of Marxist influence, the Socialists of the Chair and the Revisionists under Bernstein evidenced a more than casual interest in the work of Hess and the utopian Socialists.

After all, class cooperation, moral persuasion, and socialism through peaceful legislation and education seemed not only possible, but the most sensible course to follow in an economy which had repeatedly thwarted all of Marx's prophecies. Higher wages and other improvements of the workers' lot made it no longer seem naive to entertain hopes of peaceful and gradual progress. In any case, the Social Democrats, as Bernstein well knew, were not acting like dialectical materialists or scientific Socialists at all, but like sensible parliamentary Socialists. Bernstein merely wished to force the leaders of the greatest socialist party in the world to preach what they practiced. In the nineties even Engels did his own revising by suggesting that a proletarian revolution would not be necessary, and that socialism might come to Europe (as the Utopians had always maintained) peacefully and by legislation.[5] Engels, however, like all those who desired to be known as Marxists even as they did violence to the master's theories, refused to acknowledge that revisionism had its ideological counterpart in socialist ideas which had existed before there was any Marxism to be revised!

But old clichés never die. With some notable exceptions, Utopians like Moses Hess are at best condemned to the list of dim-eyed forerunners, hopelessly impractical. The need for a tactic of violence may have made it, if not necessary, at least excusable to bar optimism, hope, and ethical injunction from the dogmas of socialism, but that need—within Western civilization—is now gone; consequently it is no longer necessary to dismiss or patronize socialism's first representatives. It is a great testimony to the influence of Karl Marx that even though his own ideas have been discarded, his judgment of the utopian Socialists still stands in the way of any proper evaluation. Still, recent scholarship has done much to resurrect the reputation of utopian Socialists, and to re-evaluate the importance of their ideas. Today, it is true, social reformers have little to learn from men like Hess. For if socialism is now said to "creep," that is because it seems preferable to most that socialism feel its way step by step along the firm ground of experience. Neither Marx with his dialectical materialism, nor Hess with his dialectical idealism have much to say to an age so avowedly suspicious of system builders as ours. If socialism—both utopian and scientific—is superseded today, it is not because a new theoretical system has replaced these older ones but because systematic theorizing about politics and society has itself come into disrepute.

The battle between the two rival systems is over, the dust has settled, and it is now possible to see the combatants as they were. Utopian Socialists need no longer be sacrificed to the cause of world revolution, nor need Marx be made to say more or less than he intended in order to preserve his good name. The problem is one of correcting old judgments which were the product of past attitudes made obsolete by the waning of the influence of Marx and the lessening of the prestige of scientism. Any correction of ingrained judgments requires a new review of the facts and a thorough explanation of what those who have suffered under such judgments really meant to say. It is to provide both of these that the present essay has been written.

There is another and more important reason why we should experience the thought and life of one of a generation of Utopians. David Riesman has expressed it well.

A revival of the tradition of utopian thinking seems to me one of the important intellectual tasks of today. Since we live in a time of disenchantment, such thinking, where it is rational in aim and method and not mere escapism, is not easy; it is easier to concentrate on programs for choosing among lesser evils, even to the point where these evils can scarcely be distinguished, one from the other. For there is always a market for lesser-evil thinking which poses immediate alternatives; the need for thinking which confronts us with great hopes and plans is not so evident. Yet without great plans, it is hard, and often self-defeating, to make little ones.[6]

Moses Hess and the
Sacred History of Mankind

Moses Hess was the most radical utopian of all the early German Socialists, and the best known to his contemporaries. In philosophy an Idealist and in politics an anarchist, his contributions to the left-wing journals of the day set the tone for a small group known as the *True Socialists*.[1] After Marx, Engels, Rodbertus, and Weitling, Hess is the best remembered of the first German Socialists; he is still referred to as the "father of German socialism." Still, it is not his own work which gained him some measure of fame, but his influence over Marx and Engels in the forties. Hess wrote—and Gustav Mayer, the biographer of Engels, has verified it—that it was Hess who first demonstrated to Engels that left-Hegelianism led logically to communism.[2] Furthermore, it was Hess who, in 1842, recommended Marx to the editorial board of the *Rheinische Zeitung*, and who, while working on the editorial staff with Marx, first suggested to the brilliant young liberal and left-Hegelian that he should take socialism seriously and inform himself by reading the classic works of French socialism.[3] Indeed, Hess shares with Lorenz von Stein the honor of being the first to introduce French socialism to the German public.

Yet Hess has not enjoyed an enviable reputation among those who have concerned themselves with German socialism. Engels and Marx gave the cue to Marxist scholars when they denounced the ideas of Moses Hess and Karl Gruen, another True Socialist, in the *Communist Manifesto*. There Hess was accused of hiding sensible French socialist ideas behind the "fantasies" and "non-sense" of German philosophy, of ignoring the class struggle, of aiding the reactionaries, and of propagating a "filthy and enervating literature." [4] This vituperation from the founders of scientific socialism was an attack against Hess's utopian idealism; it was Hess's reward for insisting upon the efficacy of non-revolutionary moral persuasion and education as means to radical social reform. In the eyes of Marx and Engels, such "piety" could only aid the reactionaries, for it ignored the brutal reality of the class struggle and hid from the proletariat the terrible realization that they were destined to meet force with force, and could not hope to persuade. The anger of Marx and Engels was only increased, one may assume, by their awareness of the popularity of ethical, philosophical, or "true" socialism among the radicals of the *Vormaerz;* for they remarked in the *Manifesto* that almost all German socialism was utopian. Very little has been done to correct the charges Marx, Engels, and the Marxists have leveled against Hess, and the relevant literature is full of the stated or implied invective of the pseudoscientists: "incurable romantic," "hopeless Utopian," "reactionary dreamer." Such has been Hess's reward for finding his inspiration in ethical idealism rather than in "scientific" materialism.

The intense ethical idealism which was to govern the thought of Moses Hess was revealed at an early age. He was born in Bonn in 1812, the son of a Jewish businessman.[5] When he was five, his parents moved to Cologne to establish a sugar refinery, but there was no Hebrew school in Cologne and Moses stayed behind with his grandfather. From him Moses received his first instruction in the Pentateuch; many years later Moses Hess described the avidity with which he had first followed the tale of the historical mission of his people.[6] Regretfully, Moses left Bonn

for Cologne in 1825. His mother had died and his father required
help with the family business. There Moses Hess worked for the
next six years but not without making it clear to his father that
he did not choose to make a career of commerce and industry.
Pleading scholarly ambitions, he was evidently allowed to attend
the University of Bonn in 1830, although not as a registered
student.

Hess's letters from the late twenties and early thirties show
little interest in politics.[7] Even though in July of 1830 he expressed an allegiance to the principles of constitutional monarchy,
the date and tone of the letter indicate that only the pressure of
revolutionary events caused him to express liberal sentiments.
Otherwise he showed only a single-minded interest in ethics and
religion, and an addiction to pompous moral exhortation. For
example, Hess urged one of his friends to obey the divine voice
of conscience, sealed in man's nature by God in order to make
him able to create an ethical world order. Still, the letters are of
interest, for they reveal the moral sensitivity of a youth who was
to become the most radical of Utopians, and who was to decide,
in the mid-thirties, that social anarchism would be the final expression of God's will through the actions of men.

To present this thought Hess wrote, in 1836, *The Sacred History of Mankind*. He may have been stimulated by a knowledge
of French socialism gained on one of his trips to France, Belgium,
and Switzerland during the thirties. However, Hess owed less to
French socialism than any other German radical of the forties,
including Karl Marx. In fact, until the eighteen fifties, Hess found
in German philosophical idealism sufficient inspiration for the
creation of a radical ideology.

The Sacred History of Mankind is one of those vague but powerful mixtures of history, philosophy, theology, and radical idealism found among the young generation of German intellectuals
who had been influenced by German idealism during the late
thirties and early forties; such books were especially popular
among the left-Hegelians. The title reveals the familiar theme:
the history of man is sacred because it is the progressive revela-

tion of the Divine Spirit. Hess begins as Hegel began. At first sight history seems a chaos, its events apparently unrelated to one another and motivated solely by the passion, selfishness, and will to power of men. But that is mere appearance. Correctly interpreted, history reveals an ordered and rational pattern which is the obvious work of divine wisdom. "Only he who closes his eyes and ears, or is blind and deaf by nature, can deny that before and after him the Holy Spirit of God is visibly at work in history." [8]

In these words one hears echoes of the voices of Herder, Lessing, Fichte, and Hegel; yet who would come by the thought more naturally than a young Jew who had followed again and again, and always with intense interest, the fate of the chosen people driven from Egypt to Israel in fulfillment of their sacred mission in history? The German Idealists used Christ and the Reformation as symbols of the revelation of the Divine in history; Hess was able to add the ancient history of his people to the list of world-historical events. Accordingly, true to the traditional view of German philosophers from Lessing through Hegel, Hess believed philosophy to be the rationalization of theology, and history the exemplification of the truths of both. "Religion and history," he wrote in this early work, "stand in close relationship, and one explains the other." [9] Never before and rarely since has history been assigned such high rank among the sciences as it was by the intellectuals of early nineteenth century Germany. As Hess put it, history is "incontestably the science which spreads the greatest light over the social and spiritual condition of man." [10]

Still, the study of the past cannot be said to have benefited unconditionally from the attentions of those philosophers whose desire for system often made them unwilling to submit their rigorous terms to the unpatterned variety of historical events. And Hess shared that desire for system. He complained that historians have not really known history at all but have been content to chronicle what they take to be mere masses of unrelated detail and events. Like Hegel and Fichte before him, Hess conceived of history as though it were some great Being, wielding its forces and shaping its eras irresistibly through time. Forgetting for the moment the work of those from whom he himself had perhaps profited, Hess boasted: "In these pages the first attempt will be made to bring order into chaos, the first attempt to conceive of world history in her totality and order." [11] It was not lack of modesty alone which caused Hess to think of himself as a "small tool of eternal prophecy," for he was able to generalize from the ancient history of his people and he was also filled with the prophetic spirit engendered by German idealism.[12] For Hess, the historian was a prophet in the sense that he could detect the plan of the divine in the events of history. Like all radical Idealists of the *Vormaerz*, Hess tried to find far more than could be found in the story of man's past: was history not the revelation of God, the prophecy of the future and hence the key to the future of socialism?

Still in the tradition of German idealism, Hess divided man's past into three great eras. (There were, of course, others to whom Hess could have turned for precedent, for example, Saint-Simon or Fourier, but in the eighteen-thirties Hess was not sufficiently acquainted with their work.) To those who have an extensive knowledge of the past, all attempts at a rigid periodization of the past will appear, if not arbitrary, at least uniformed. But it would be fruitless to judge Hess's view of history by the canons of historical criticism alone. Hess was no historian and disdained the empirical standards upheld by those who retell the events of the past; he would not allow "mere facts" to dim his vision. It is best, then, to judge such schemes by the motives and the vision which inspire them rather than by the gross oversimplifications which they propagate. And Hess's purpose is clear. He wanted to demonstrate to his reader that the perfect society would be the certain culmination of history, and he wanted to communicate some part of the enthusiasm which overwhelmed him when he first realized that the good society had behind it all the force of divine necessity.

The scheme of history employed by Moses Hess was, of course, constructed according to dialectical principles and—as is common to all those who attach theological meaning to the dialectic—Hess found great significance in the number three.

> What is born in time develops itself in three periods. In the first period it takes root, forms a unity, and lives internally—that is the root of life. In the second period it grows, is divided and lives externally—that is the crown of life. In the third it waxes, is united again and ripens—that is the fruit of life.[13]

This is the familiar dialectical movement of thesis, antithesis, and synthesis, expressed by an analogy with the organic world, and altered to read: original unity, followed by disunity, and culminating in a final and "higher" unity. And the terms of this version of the dialectical process were, for Hess, the ideal and the real. Through this analogy, Hess wished to introduce the notion that in world history the ideal and the real were first united, then separated, and, finally, united once more in the final scene, as it were, of man's drama on earth.

Accordingly, Hess divided the past into three eras, each with its appropriate world-historical figure: Adam, Christ, and Spinoza. In the first period, Hess continued, man was a unity, in that Adam was unaware of any conflict between hope and fact or the ideal and the real—it was a time of unconscious innocence and perfection unearned. But Adam desired and sinned; with this came a knowledge of the insufficiency of reality. Torn between desire, conscience, and dissatisfaction, Adam was doomed to "struggle restlessly for his lost treasure," the original unity of his soul.[14]

With the birth of Christ, then, man entered the second great era of his history, characterized by the radical separation of the ideal and real. In politics and society, brute force and lawless strife were the rule. "The Gospels were concerned only with the spirit. In Christianity, religion was separated from politics. The Christians had no social order grounded in God, no holy state, and no sacred law." [15] During the Christian era, the ideal did not find expression in the real; still, it was then that the ideal itself was created. In the quiet isolation of the monastery and in the pure souls of perfect Christians the highest virtues of perfect idealism were nurtured. And it was necessarily so, argued Hess, for only when man is unhindered by the pressures and temptations of the material world can he find the ideal. During the Christian era, the spirit "sunk itself into the depths of its own soul and searched and grubbed until it found the truth." [16] It found and founded, for Christian idealism, created in the Middle Ages and guided by the perfect virtue of Christ's message, was destined to reshape the external world.

In the third era—symbolized by Spinoza—the soul is fated to shape the world according to its own image of perfection.

> With Spinoza began nothing less than the time which He [Christ] and His first disciples had desired, hoped for, and prophesied. The time of the Holy Ghost began, the Empire of God, the New Jerusalem. It was the time of that other world, the contemplation of which had given comfort to every true Christian.[17]

Spinoza's writings had acted with all the force of a divine revelation on the young Hess, and he expressed his debt in the subtitle of *The Sacred History of Mankind: by a Disciple of Spinoza*. The Jew of Amsterdam had taught the unity of the ideal and the real, and in this Hess found the theme of the third and final era of history. In the third era, men will unite the divine and the secular, spirit and matter, by creating a society in which the ideal has been made real. Since Christ, Hess remarked, Christian dualism has taught men to think of the spirit *versus* matter, faith *or* reason, and the ideal *as opposed to* the real. Spinoza dissolved Christian dualism with the powerful acid of his pantheism; God is everywhere, God is all, and, correspondingly, all distinction between the divine and the secular and the real and the ideal has been removed. Spinoza's metaphysics could not be resisted by a radical idealist who was certain that there were no limits to the creative powers of man.

It is unusual to find a dialectical Idealist who is inspired by

Spinoza as well as by Hegel or Fichte. Zlocisti remarked that Hess, like so many young Jewish intellectuals of the day, learned his Latin from Spinoza and his German from Hegel.[18] Hess did not read Fichte until after the publication of his first book, and Hegel's wise reluctance to expect too much from men could not satisfy one possessed of such a fiery sense of divine mission. After all, Hegel was convinced that pure spirit would never find adequate expression in society and politics, but must be content to reign in art, religion, and philosophy. For the metaphysics of the perfect society, then, Hess turned to Spinoza. By so doing Hess did not think he was turning away from Hegel; rather, Hess regarded pantheism as the completion of the Hegelian dialectic: if history is the story of the gradual realization of the Divine in the affairs of men, must not the goal of history be a pantheistic unity of the divine and the secular? Of course, Spinoza's pantheism was meant as a description of being and not as a prophecy of the future, but Hess's enthusiasm would not let him respect the "master's" wishes in this. Hess placed Spinoza's pantheism at the end of the dialectical process Hegel had taught him to observe in history. "The time nears," Hess concluded, "when the once destroyed original unity will be re-established, when the state will again become holy, and when the empire of God will appear." [19]

In the latter half of the *Sacred History of Mankind* Hess was concerned with history in the making, not history made. For the "third era" was not yet over, its future—if decided—was not yet worked out. Consequently, Hess indicated briefly the ways in which Spinoza's vision of the unity of the ideal and the real was being worked out in the course of events which had occurred since the "master" had first announced the theme of the era. Hess cited the achievements of the French Enlightenment; for the first time, he maintained, the standards of idealism were used to criticize the state and society. The Enlightenment sounded the prelude to the modern age. With the *philosophes* we witness:

Not a deluge of water, as after Adam, nor a deluge of peoples,

as after Christ, but a deluge of ideas which climbs threaten-
ingly up out of the womb of time to rage against that which
blocks its way.[20]

To prove the inevitability of the perfect society, Hess thought
it sufficient to show man's desire for it and his ability to conceive
of it. Ideas were for him the supreme force, and once man had
taken up the notion of social reform, the outcome was certain.
He felt no need to argue the point. For him as for all the Forty-
eighters it was a simple fact that man makes history just as the
spirit moves him.

> . . . according to the same laws and in the same order as the
> individual's spirit, or his inner history, keeps equal steps with
> his body, or his external history, so also in the history of man-
> kind the external development goes hand in hand with the
> inner spiritual development.[21]

It is foolish, Hess continued, to blame the ruling classes of past
centuries for the misery of the lower orders; had men not been
slaves and serfs in spirit during the past they could never have
been so treated. Correspondingly, the Enlightenment and the
French Revolution prove that men are no longer willing to submit to autocracy. As for the Restoration, it cannot succeed, for the
old spirit of man cannot be restored.

To believe so strongly in progress that one is continually
tempted to speak of it as "inevitable" does not prevent one from
condemning one's own time as the worst: Fichte's writings illus-
trate this. Hess expressed his pessimism about the condition of
Europe by prefacing his *Sacred History of Mankind* with a three-
page quotation from Jacoby's *The Complaint of a Jew*. In this
poem, Europe is compared to a decaying and rotten corpse, foul
and fit only for burial. Hess quoted it and believed it, yet he did
not think himself inconsistent. Of course, he explained, men are
better off than ever before, but that is not the point. "For even if
. . . external conditions were once much worse than now, the
inner spirit suited them. That is not so with us, and that is the
great evil of our time." [22] It was precisely this sense of contrast

between what Europe was and what she might be that caused so
many to use the dialectical method of philosophic idealism. All
the Romanticists of the "Age of Metternich" were singularly
aware of the contrast between hope and fact. For German radicals, the real and the ideal did seem as radically separated as the
dialectical method demands, while their optimism and hope
made them think that nevertheless, the realm of the ideal was
more than equal to its task of reshaping the real.

Man's misery in our day, Hess continued, is caused by the
inadequacy of his material conditions of existence when seen in
the light of his ideal aspirations. Still, Hess had very little to say
in his first book about those staples of socialist thought—especially after 1850—the laws of economics. Only three pages of the
Sacred History of Mankind are used to communicate the misery
of the proletariat and the rapacity of the bourgeoisie.[23] Hess
thought it more important to dwell on the ethical reasons and
impulses which would bring about the reform of "mere" conditions. Not until the late forties did Hess turn his attention to the
power of the laws of economics and then only after his faith in
moral persuasion had somewhat lessened.

In 1836 Hess did mention some of the more well-known principles of socialist criticism of the capitalist system: the increasing
concentration of capital in the hands of a moneyed aristocracy,
the decimation of the guilds and small business classes by the
unregulated competition raging between industrial giants, and
the tendency for the rich to become richer and the poor, poorer.
Hess accepted these notions as matters of fact and made no attempt to test them with the realities of economic change. His
refusal to stake the future of socialism on the force of economic
law may, perhaps, be accepted in partial mitigation of his care-
lessness. For him, in any event, the material existence of man—
his economic, political, and social conditions—contradicted shock-
ingly the advanced moral spirit of the era of Spinoza.

For [these institutions] were based on a limited spirit of man
which was incapable of protecting private property without

prejudicing personal service; which could not maintain the order of the whole without lessening the freedom of the individual; which could not make obedience sacred without engendering a blind faith in authority . . . which could not spur the activity of men without the stimulus of base selfishness, or enthuse its heroes without the spur of ambition; which could not make self-denial divine without holding out the hope of other-worldly rewards . . . and could not even disseminate a knowledge of God without the services of a paid priest-class.[24]

Hess's lack of interest in the institutions of society and the laws of economics was not mere ignorance. It was, rather, a result of his idealism and a stimulus to it. He did not admit the force of laws and institutions. The spirit is supreme and society is but its manifestation; believing this, he thought it sufficient to indicate what the best thought and highest moral claims of men demand of society. His hope and enthusiasm led him to believe that when that has been done the outlines of the society of the future must stand revealed.

It was this extreme idealism, this refusal to recognize any claims but those of the spirit, which caused Hess to become the most radical Socialist of the German *Vormaerz*. In the community of goods without private property—which many radicals had denounced as too visionary—Hess found a hint of the future. "Let us recognize the service of those who have spoken the significant word *Guetergemeinschaft*," he wrote, "for they have pointed out to us the final goal of social life." [25]

Even the most egalitarian society heretofore conceived could not satisfy one whose vision of the future was inspired by Spinoza's pantheism. Where property is divided equally and held in common, some group would have to divide the property, and law and force would have to be used to maintain the division. And Hess wanted no law and no force and no distinction whatsoever between ownership and work, ruler and ruled, law and free act; all such "contradictions" between the real and the ideal must be washed away in the ocean of Divine Being, and in a society of self-regulating men.

> For the old contradictions between lower and higher, plebeian and patrician, poor and rich—this source of all collisions, disturbances, injustices, and cruelties—they have lost their power in the Holy Empire. In the Empire of God such contradictions are no longer dangerous because they smooth themselves out in a natural way, disappear more and more with every day, and in the end will be gone completely and utterly.[26]

Hess concluded that there would be such a society because man's ethical consciousness will become a part of divinity itself. Man will know and want perfection and will have no need for direction. "What need will there be . . . for an external law for the whole, when the law lives inside it?"[27] Other radicals might stop somewhere along the road to perfection; Hess would not stop until he found God in man and the perfect order of perfect anarchy. How Hegel would have shuddered at the sight of this youth pushing the thought that history is the realization of the Divine to its final conclusion!

> In the most distant future . . . there will come forth no new law, because mankind will be as united in spirit as they will be equal externally; the law of God will live in every limb and will be known with utter clarity.[28]

Hess gave no further details of life in the perfect society, nor could he, perhaps, for there would be no laws and institutions to describe. He thought it enough to indicate that man would one day regain the original unity of the age of Adam—the unity between desire and act, and will and conscience; and this within the framework of communial egalitarianism.

One cannot dispute a vision or argue with a prophet, and words can do little against such extremes of enthusiasm. The best one can do, perhaps, is to understand. Even for a radical of the eighteen-forties, Hess expected too much from mind and morality to avoid being called a visionary by fellow radicals of his own day. In his answer to the charge, one senses the way in which German metaphysics gave comfort to those appalled by German politics. "The idea of the future is still locked in the spirit of the times

and has certainly not yet found its world; but it already has a
spiritual history and that speaks clearly enough." [29] If one cannot
share Hess's vision of the future, one can at least treat it seriously,
if not for itself, then because Hess was willing to stake his future
on its truth. When Hess left his father's business in Cologne to
become a publicist for the third era, he traded security and comfort for the faint hope of converting men to a new ideal and
showed the kind of nerve that makes idealism compelling and
attractive however wrongheaded. For Hess had not chosen a safe
task or an easy career, nor one which seemed to offer any chance
of success. It was a leap in the dark. There were no political
parties to be led, no political careers to be had, and as if that
were not enough, no electorate to be persuaded. Hess launched
himself upon a life of cheap rooms, bad food, and constant debt,
with his very freedom threatened by the ever-present police agent
patiently waiting just across the border. It meant that Hess must
be continually on the move, writing brief articles, made briefer
by the red pencil of the censor, for short-lived journals whose
appearance was always doubtful and whose circulation at best
could usually be numbered in the hundreds. Such was the life
he chose. And though the fires of his enthusiasm did burn low on
occasion, they never burnt out. "As far as we are concerned, we
will from now on unfold before the eyes of our contemporaries
the basic idea of modern times, and, where it is necessary, defend it from stupid or ill-willed attacks." [30]

The True Socialist

In September of 1841, Hess found his first chance to start a career in journalism. George Jung, left-Hegelian and liberal, asked Hess to help sell shares in a newspaper published in Cologne, the *Rheinische Allegemeine Zeitung.* Jung also wanted Hess to join the editorial staff; the paper was not paying for itself and its owners hoped to revive it by selling shares and recruiting fresh talent. Hess welcomed Jung's offer, and hoped to transform the paper into a sounding board for German radical idealism. Since the publication of his second book in 1841, *The European Triarchy,* Hess had won a favorable reputation among the liberals and radicals of the Berlin circle of left-Hegelians: among others, Marx, Engels, Arnold Ruge, Bruno Bauer, Friedrich Koeppen, and Karl Nauwerk. Until the publication of the first issue in January 1842—renamed the *Rheinische Zeitung*—Hess and Jung played the most active roles in the venture.[1]

The Rhineland was an excellent location for a liberal newspaper. There, as a result of the rule of the French during the Napoleonic era, feudal burdens and the privileges of the nobility had been lessened and Germany's most thriving industrial and

commercial bourgeoisie had gained equality of citizenship and a
unified and liberal system of commercial, civil, and criminal law.
Furthermore, the government of Prussia looked favorably upon
the new venture, for it was not aware of the radical intentions of
the new staff and hoped to see some competition offered to the
Koelnische Zeitung, which was too Austrian and pro-Catholic for
the pietistic traditionalists surrounding Frederick William IV. It
seemed evident that the radicals would not maintain control of
the *Rheinische Zeitung,* because most of the shares were bought
by members of the liberal bourgeoisie of the Rhineland. The government was not mistaken; though Jung had promised Hess the
post of editor-in-chief, at a stormy meeting of the stockholders'
representatives in December, 1841, the men of commerce and
industry made it quite clear that Germany's first Communist
would not direct the policies of their paper. Constitutional monarchy, free enterprise, the *Zollverein,* and equality for the bourgeois in Prussia—in short, liberal criticism without radical sub-
version—were the aims of the owners. And they had their way.
At no time before the last month of its existence (March 1843)
was the paper receptive to socialism. Even its last and most successful editor, Karl Marx, looked with a baleful eye on the visions
of the radical left. Hess, although influential among the editorial
staff, of which he was a member, had to be content with supervis-
ing the reporting of French affairs. From December of 1842 until
the last issue, that of April 1, 1843, he sent his articles to Cologne
from Paris, as French correspondent of the *Rheinische Zeitung.*

Hess was not discouraged; after all, the task of representing
Paris on one of the leading German liberal newspapers was con-
genial. Here he began his long career as mediator between the
two forces which, he had insisted in the *European Triarchy,*
would dominate and shape the modern era—French socialism and
German philosophy. Like all left-Hegelians of the *Vormaerz,*
Hess admired what he regarded as the French talent for making
revolutions and the German ability to create revolutionary phi-
losophies. As mediator between France and Germany, might he
not bring Hegel to Paris and Babeuf to Berlin? To Hess, as to

Fichte, the role of each nation in history seemed to have the clarity of the preordained. "The speculative German lives in the ideal," he wrote, "while the action-loving Frenchman works in the real." [2]

In other ways and with far too great ease, Hess was able to fit the "national characteristics" of the French and Germans into his grand prophetic scheme for the third era. For example, he made spirited analogies between Napoleon and Goethe, Robespierre and Fichte, the French Revolution and the German Reformation. It was Hess's hope that the political activism of the French would bring about the realization of the spiritual values worked into system and theory by the German Idealists.

> In France freedom was finally brought to life, and while France bloodily fought to victory, Germany's greatest men, from Kant and Schiller to Goethe and Hegel, sat in their studies and celebrated a similar victory—of the spirit.[3]

Hess saw in each nation's achievements an expression of the familiar dualisms of German philosophy: Germany and France, the ideal and the real, theory and practice, philosophy and politics. Thinking as he did, Hess could hardly have found a more fruitful task than that of explaining the virtues of one country to the intellectuals of another. Hess saw himself as the mediator between the sundered halves of the world-spirit, and he enjoyed contemplating the mighty power for social reform which would be unleashed if those halves could ever join in a common European task. Could he himself not be at once Fichte and Babeuf, and could there be a more subversive combination? Hess could think of none, and in the pages of *The European Triarchy* he insisted that world socialism could find no better weapon than one combining the virtues of the great expounder of the world as creative moral ego and the first modern organizer of revolutionary secret societies.

Hess was not so foolish as to reveal his ultimate allegiance to the Prussian censors or the Rhenish bourgeoisie, for upon them depended the future of his hopes and the fate of the *Rheinische*

Zeitung. Like a true mediator, he played a careful game. He tried
to lull the readers of the Rhineland's best hope into a state of
receptivity to socialism by suggesting in his articles that, after
all, one must be a Socialist if one admired the liberal reforms
brought by Napoleon to the Rhineland. Working on the Rhenish
bourgeosie's allegiance to at least the expressed ideals of the first
year of the French Revolution, Hess tried to suggest that even
the complete victory of the middle classes of France had not yet
led to the realization of those ideals.[4] Often Hess used the
familiar technique of presenting a flattering view of socialist ideas
as merely the latest curiosities of Paris and therefore worthy of
report. Or again, when discussing the advantages and disadvan-
tages of centralizing the power of the state, Hess was careful to
appeal to the average industrialist's desire for a unified Germany;
but if the bourgeois were thinking of a national German *Zollverein,* Hess was thinking of the ease with which a unified state
could expropriate the expropriators.[5] He also asked his readers
to consider whether any state power at all would be necessary if
men were really as just and righteous as they should be—and
probably will be in the future, he added. "The central power
would then reside in each limb, as is actually the case with
every healthy organism." [6] It would not do to suggest any more
clearly than that his ultimate goal of anarchism, and Hess did
not labor the point.

Continuing his attempt to turn the liberal industrialists into
radicals, Hess argued that they were not aware of the latest
truths as revealed in England—then as usual the model for German liberals—and insisted that in England "everyone knows" that
"mere" political reforms are no longer sufficient to solve the problems of society. The concentration of capital in the hands of a
ruthless *Geldaristokratie,* and the progressive oppression of the
proletariat, he continued, are not problems which can be solved
by constitutional changes.[7] Hess even had a word of advice for
the Prussian censors, and here he slyly turned the platitudes of
the common *Spiessbuerger* to uncommon use. In Germany, he
wrote, ideas rarely have consequences because Germans are sat-

isfied with passive speculation and do not demand action as do the French. Consequently, press censorship while perhaps necessary in France, is quite superfluous in Germany. In later years this bit of slyness on the part of a young and optimistic radical was to become the haunting fear of an old and disappointed revolutionist, finally convinced that his people did not have it in them to erect barricades. In the early forties, however, Hess was not yet discouraged, even though he was aware that his advice was not acceptable to either the Prussian censors or the German bourgeoisie.

Hess's cleverest attempt to persuade the readers of the *Rheinische Zeitung* in favor of his revolutionary pantheism, appeared in an article in which he discussed the difference between religion and morality.[8] It would have been foolish to attack established religions directly in pietistic Prussia and the Rhineland—then as ever the stronghold of German Catholicism. In order to raise doubts instead of a wall of dogmatic rejection, Hess had to proceed carefully yet make his point: that religion cannot aid in the reform of society. For, Hess wrote, one prays *to* God, and one appeals from the suffering of earthly life to the promise of bliss in eternal life. Hence, he continued, the "theological consciousness" finds necessary a radical distinction between the divine and the secular, and subordinates earthly life to a God outside and a world beyond. To be religious is to purge oneself of this world in preparation for the next. It is the great and worthy task of religion to give comfort to the weak, he implied, but it cannot aid the strong to improve the here and now. Moral consciousness, Hess wrote, is something else again. It is the awareness of the unity of the divine and the secular, and it creates the desire to form that unity in society and politics. Sharpening his attack, Hess asked, how can priests and their flock be of any help to social reform when they assume human knowledge to be as nothing and the human will but a vain delusion?

Those who are tempted to dismiss as superficial Hess's view of the social role of religion should remember the reactionary force of the pietistic Lutheran clergy in Prussia and the conservative

ultramontanism of the Catholic clergy in the Rhineland. Then
too, Hess protested against the Christian view of divinity precisely because he felt the reform of society to be a divine duty;
he hoped to gain converts for the invisible church of Spinoza's
pantheism. Later in life, when he thought it no longer possible
to persuade the faithful to seek divinity in this world, he replaced
careful persuasion with simple denunciation and finally agreed
with Marx that religion was no more than the opium of the
people.

In spite of his care, Hess was given little opportunity to smuggle his anarchism into the world-view of the burghers of Cologne;
even Marx's liberalism was too radical for the Prussian government. By the spring of 1843, those in the Prussian cabinet who
all along had hoped to stifle the *Rheinische Zeitung* had their
way, and the paper was suppressed in April. Marx left for Paris.
Liberalism was to be allowed no voice in the Hohenzollern fief.
In this way the representatives of Frederick William IV encour-
aged the very radicalism they feared. Paris in the forties had
already become the second home of German radicals, and there
many of them, like Marx, exchanged their liberalism for socialism, and so found weapons more capable of causing sleepless
nights for the unenlightened despots who had driven them out.

Hess, of course, was a Socialist before he arrived in Paris. He
was there to convert, not to be converted. And in spite of the
closing of the *Rheinische Zeitung*, he had not given up his hope
of reaching the German public. While in Paris he met the leaders of radical secret societies whose members were recruited
from among the seventy thousand or so German artisans who
were working in Paris in order to meet the travel requirements
of their guilds.[9] The two most important of these societies called
themselves the Union of the Righteous and the Union of the
Despised. Both attempted to smuggle radical literature into
Germany. Hess made a point of attending their meetings, for he
thought he might gain converts to his social anarchism and, more
important, reach the German public through them.

The artisans had little knowledge of political theory and philosophy, and were easily impressed by the erudition of the "young Hegelian communist philosopher from Rhenish Prussia," as they called him.[10] Wilhelm Weitling, the erratic, passionate tailor from Germany and Switzerland, had considerable influence among them, and his powerful moral idealism and frank utopianism can be traced in their *Manifestos* and *Addresses*. With lavish use of biblical phraseology, they wrote of their desire for brotherhood and equality, and hinted darkly at the future abolition of private property. They carried on their deliberations filled with cheap wine and heady with religiosity, but in spite of all excesses they gave life to the moral imperatives. To Hess they must have seemed more promising material than the bourgeoisie of the Rhineland. They were, after all, the only German workingmen that Hess or any other Socialist was able to excite before the advent of the brilliant Lassalle.

To the radicals of Paris, Hess, like so many German Socialists of the day, hoped to bring the discipline of German philosophy. Hess criticized the "one-sided evangelicalism" of the German guildsmen of Paris as well as French Utopians in general. "Socialism," he wrote, "is not only the highest religion, it is also the highest science [*Wissenschaft*]; although Socialists should be apostles, they must also be philosophers if they are to reach their goals." [11] Of course, Hess was not thinking, as Marx would later, of the science of political economy, but of the philosophy of dialectical idealism. Still, Hess was perhaps responding to the same impulse as Marx, when he hoped to replace French "sentimentality" with stern, "Germanic" system. For the French, Hess charged, socialism is merely sentiment and sympathy, they have no awareness of the philosophy of the spirit in history which makes of socialism a systematic and theoretical science. Like Marx, Hess hoped to persuade his French colleagues that socialism was not only morally desirable but historically inevitable. To the heirs of Babeuf, Saint-Simon, and Fourier, he hoped to transmit the heritage of Fichte and Hegel: ". . . the total unity of German theory with French practice will make perfect socialism possible." [12]

In his second book, *The European Triarchy* (1841), Hess had taken the first step toward uniting the virtues of the two nations by attempting the conversion of German Idealists into French Revolutionists. In the Foreword he announced his goal: "German philosophy has fulfilled its mission, it has led us to the truth. Now it is up to us to build bridges leading from heaven to earth." [13] The philosophy of the spirit, Hess became fond of repeating, must become a philosophy of the act.[14] The attitude is familiar now and was well-known in the early forties: heretofore, philosophers have only observed the world, it is our task to change it. Marx made the slogan famous among a later generation, but he was not the one who first expressed it. Indeed, the radical Idealists of the early forties were united by the hope that one day the idealism of the philosophers would be built into a new political and social order, and Marx merely based that hope on a different foundation—the laws of economics and the class struggle. And Hess, in the *Sacred History of Mankind,* had already called for the realization of the values of German idealism in society. The brilliant young Polish nobleman and Idealist, August von Cieszkowski, had offered, in his *Prolegomena zur Historisophie* (1838), the first systematic attempt to transform Hegelianism into a radical philosophy of social reform, and Hess gave him full credit.[15]

With Cieszkowski and the young Hegelians, and against the "old" or "right" Hegelians, who thought they had found in Hegel a defender of the petty despots of Prussia, Hess insisted that the philosophy of Hegel contradicted the presumed politics of Hegel:

> Only unphilosophical minds could so misunderstand Hegel; for after he, in his *Phenomenology,* caused all manifestations of the spirit—as finite—to find destruction in the infinity of self-consciousness, and after he, in his *Logic,* described the eternal forms of self-consciousness as the only truths: after all this, how could mere historical and transient truths have for him any permanent, fixed, or positive validity? Nowhere does Hegelian philosophy recognize anything as permanent or final, excluding only the work of the spirit which out of itself—the

eternal source of all truth—must bring forth and constantly re-
new all truth.

Nor is it just, continued Hess, to accuse Hegel of conservatism
merely because he did not use his philosophy as a critical weapon
against the social order of his day. It was his task to bring philosophy to completion; he had enough of a struggle: "to make the
spirit adequate to itself, that which remained, to shape life so as
to be adequate to the spirit, he had to leave to others." [16]

Still, there was much in Hegel's philosophy of the spirit which
a radical bent on social reform could not accept. Hegel, for example, had explained the past, but he had refused to divine the
future. Moreover, Hegel had denied the possibility of foreknowl-
edge of the future manifestations of the spirit, and this, to his
radical followers, meant condemning action to the realm of
chance and accident. With the impatience of all Utopians when
confronted with pragmatic hesitation, Hess insisted that a philosophy which could show Reason at work in the past could help
make the future reasonable by giving men a guide to the perfect
society. Indeed, Hess insisted on prediction.

> It is an essential part of the knowledge of history that out of
> the past and the present—out of that which has been and that
> which is—out of these two known quantities to deduce an un-
> known third, that which is becoming, the future. So seen, the
> task of the philosophy of history is one worthy of it, and when
> that task is finished the philosophy of history will become the
> philosophy of the act.[17]

Hess and the left-Hegelians were too radical to accept Hegel's
belief in the mystery of a divine creation whose works could be
contemplated but not foreseen. Even the contemplation of the
Divine was not enough for Hess and the activists of the *Vormaerz*.
The desire for certainty where there could be none, i.e., as to the
future of history, was a part of Hess's enthusiastic unwillingness
to condemn the future of socialism to the realm of the merely
probable.

Accordingly, it was Hegel's transcendentalism which presented the greatest barrier to the reformist impulses of Hess and the left-Hegelians, and caused them to reject him even as they accepted him. They would not believe, with Hegel, that the great movements of history were the form taken by the transcendental Absolute as it realized itself in time. For Hegel, of course, man does the work of the spirit, but he knows not what he does, and he acts without any knowledge of the true purpose and final results of his actions—this is the "cunning of reason." Were Hess to accept Hegel's transcendentalism, he would have to surrender his utopian faith in the power of man's conscious efforts to bring about the good society, and he would have to admit, with Hegel, that man cannot hope to participate wittingly in the creation of the divine on earth, but must content himself with contemplation of the history of the Spirit in the past—the philosopher's task, according to Hegel. And there would be little point in formulating a philosophy of the act, for of what importance are the actions of men to those seeking to understand the grand scheme of a world which, in conception, existence, and goal, owes nothing to the plans of men?

Hess had already found an alternative to Hegel's transcendental dualism in Spinoza's theory of the unity of the divine and the secular: for if man is part of the divine, it follows that he is capable of participating in the plan of the divine. Before Hess understood the full implications of this notion with regard to Hegelianism, however, Ludwig Feuerbach had presented his critique of Hegel's Christian dualism; and in Feuerbach's work Hess and the left-Hegelians found the first philosophic defense of their belief in the unlimited creative possibilities of man.[18] Feuerbach denied the existence of a God beyond the experience and world of man. God is man's creation; man is the only creator in the world, and there is no higher spiritual authority before which man need humble himself. Such a clear statement of utopian humanism could not fail to inspire Hess. After Feuerbach, Hess insisted, it must be obvious that nothing bars man from achieving all that his ideals and hopes have led him to desire, for

Feuerbach has shown that man is the creator of God, history, and society. Precisely because he had been searching, since the publication of his first work, for the means with which to correct Hegel's dualism in the light of Spinoza's pantheism, Hess was one of the first to recognize Feuerbach's service and to feel free to transform Hegelianism into a radical philosophy of social action and reform.

It is difficult for us to imagine now, perhaps, the tremendous relief and enthusiasm with which the radical Idealists of the eighteen-forties greeted Feuerbach's humanism. It is not too much to say that next to Hegel, Feuerbach was the most influential philosopher of the *Vormaerz*. It took thirty years for German philosophy to move from Christian dualism to the humanism of Feuerbach, and only with Feuerbach's critique of Hegel were the clear implications of such a break understood. That faith in human capabilities which a Saint-Simon or Fourier could freely assume, and which most of us rarely question, was hard won in Germany and was gained by men like Hess only at the cost of a long struggle with the greatest creative works of German philosophy, works which had inspired them to begin the struggle in the first place. For most of its history, German idealism was—in the best sense—a rationalization of theology. German idealism, wrote Nietzsche, is the shadow of God; God is dead, he continued, but his shadow still prevents Germans from seeing reality. And it took Feuerbach, in many ways similar to Nietzsche, to liberate young German radicals from the fear of God and Hegel, and to teach them that they might create a secular, critical, and utopian social ideal with some hope that man might benefit.

Strengthened by Spinoza and inspired by Feuerbach, Hess announced in the first sentence of Chapter One of the *European Triarchy:* "We step into a new world, into the world of the absolute spiritual act." [19] Returning to the theme of his first work, Hess insisted upon the divinity of history; history is sacred not only because it is the revelation of the Divine Spirit in time, but also because man himself is that Spirit. Was not the French Revolution, Hess continued, the first free and conscious deed of man,

and as men increasingly come to understand that they are the
only creators, will they not have the courage and will to shape
a world fit for the highest ideals of the spirit? The French Revolution was the boundary between the past and the present; before then the spirit could observe, and it could contemplate, but
after that it must act, "Our element is the ethical." [20] Again the
influence of Fichte, though unacknowledged, seems decisive in
the thought of Moses Hess. Hegel regarded the French Revolution as the victory of reason; with Fichte, Hess called it the victory of morality. The difference is crucial. Reason can, if it must,
remain content with knowledge and speculation, but the moralist
must always be driven by the impulse to act. Hegel had to be
satisfied with the thought that the spirit might find its fulfillment
in art, religion, and philosophy; Fichte and Hess had to insist on
the unrestricted activity of morality and its creation of a moral
world order. For them, socialism was *the* moral imperative, and
the irresistible consequence of man's moral impulses. To those
who denied the supremacy of man's creative moral ego, Hess
called out:

> We must shape our future ourselves. Outside of our own free
> and conscious activity we have nothing more to expect. Our
> education is over; we have grown beyond the harsh discipline
> of the law and the authority of the church. Thrown back on
> ourselves, placed on our own feet, we still stumble, as though
> hardly used to standing alone. But He who, until today, has
> stood by us, will now work in us. God is no longer our strict
> judge nor even our mild teacher, He is a spirit which is in us.
> And if we follow the urgings of this spirit, then—however far
> the goal and however tiring the way—we will never despair of
> the eventual success of our efforts.[21]

Still, even such statements as this do not reveal the intensity of
Hess's faith in the power of mind. Indeed, he believed mind to
be the only force and even the only reality, and to prove this he
intended to write a book to be called the *Philosophy of the Act.*
The book was never completed but Hess published the Introduction to it in 1843.[22] Hess began by repeating and reinterpreting

an ancient criticism of Descartes' *cogito ergo sum*, i.e., it is not possible to prove the existence of objective being from the mere fact of man's mental activity. To know *I think*, Hess wrote, is not to know *I am*, nor is it legitimate to conclude therefrom that things are. "The first, and last, that I know is my mental activity, my knowing." [23] From the existence of thought alone, Hess continued, we cannot deduce the physical existence of ourselves or the objects of our thought. Most often, of course, this criticism of Descartes' formula has been used to show that Cartesianism cannot account for the real world of objects; Hess used it, however, to deny that such a real world exists! The world about us, this most radical of Utopians insisted, is nothing more than the manifestation of the human spirit. Do not look at the world to see what is there, he argued, for the world is but a mirror reflecting man's image.[24]

Correspondingly, Hess continued, this error of assuming the existence of a real world independent of man's mind (the error of philosophical and theological dualism) has caused man to think of himself and his ideals as limited and even conditioned by the laws and forces of a world outside. In this manner, man has voluntarily surrendered his own creativity, and given obeisance to the principle of all slavery, which is the belief that man does not rule without rivals. Correctly seen, Hess insisted, man's ideals are not negated by the real world; rather, man himself has been his own negation. And once man has become aware of this, what is to stop him from becoming the negation of the negation?

> [The spirit of man] creates its opposite—the other, the world, life—in order that man may go beyond this destiny, this limit to his selfhood, and so return to himself, aware that he has met nothing less but *his* opposite, his deed, and *his* life.[25]

In this manner Hess declared his belief in an ontology of pure spirit fully capable of serving as a philosophical counterpart to his social anarchism. Here is the philosophy of social anarchism, which is itself the ultimate standard by which the imperfections of society can be measured. No philosopher and no radical has ever shown more faith in the creative possibilities open to man; in Hess's view all limits to man's power are but self-imposed errors of thought. Hess's ontology of the pure spirit is the ultimate moral claim on society, rationalized into theoretical system.

Willing to banish matter from the universe, anxious to prove the world full of pure spirit alone, Hess broke with the dialectical process as understood by the German philosophical Idealists. According to this view, change occurs because of opposition and struggle between two forces mutually conditioning one another: Spirit and matter, idea and reality, man and nature; the forces may be variously named, but as long as the dualism is maintained and *Geist* is supreme, the traditional German Idealist's view of the dialectical process has not been violated. When one of the two forces, however, is so completely dominated by the other as to have its very existence threatened or even denied, the dialectic of German philosophical idealism has been discarded. Hess denied the autonomy of the world of matter. Marx's attempt to deny the autonomy of ideas is but the reverse side of the coin; it may be as much a product of an excess of despair as the other is of an excess of hope.

As presented by Fichte and Hegel, the dialectical process was of little use to either Hess or Marx. For Hess, the dialectical process took place not between mental and material forces, but between mental forces alone—that is to say, between man's ideas and his awareness of the omnipotence of his ideas or spirit; for Hess, self-awareness is all. For Marx, however, the dialectical process took place between material forces—the mode of production and the social relationships to which that mode of production gives rise versus a new mode of production and the consequent new set of social relationships struggling to be born. Ideas were at best, for Marx, laggards behind the true forces of society and never independent of them.[26]

Of course, Hess did not direct his idealism against materialists, for few were evident among the radicals of the eighteen forties. Instead he denounced those whom he held responsible for metaphysical dualism, the theologians and philosophers. They are the ones most responsible for weakening man's will to reform, he declared, for they have divided being into two forces—the ideal and the real—and have propagated the myth of the omnipotent "other." Returning to a theme he had considered in the *Rheinische Zeitung*, Hess declared: "The theological consciousness is the great lie, the principle of all bondage (and despotism), and our race will be subject to it . . . as long as it does not recognize and value the self-conscious act." [27] As he had insisted in the *European Triarchy*:

> The old church is dead because men no longer need her. From now on the religion of love will be revealed in the works of active men and not in didactic spirituality. And we who struggle to make the state holy, to bring institutions to full perfection, to ban misery, and to unite all the contradictions and divisions of life, we—as true mediators—can boast more of our Christianity than can the members of a church stiffened into dead formalism, or a Confession grown rigid through dogmatic spirituality. [28]

And it is no accident, continued Hess, that absolute religion—Christianity—and the absolute state—divine right monarchy—are to be found together in history, and that those who defend the one usually justify the other. [29] By preaching the otherness of pure disembodied spirit, both theologians and philosophers have taught men to expect nothing from this world and everything from the next; hence men submit willingly to the despotism of the absolute state. Once men were so vicious, Hess conceded, that it was necessary to frighten them with the power of such "general abstractions" (a term Hess acquired from Feuerbach), but man's awareness of his moral nature has increased so much that he no longer needs to submit to the awesome but imagined power of God and King. "Religion and politics are but bridges which mark the transition from unawareness to self-awareness of the spirit." [30] Throughout history, Hess declared, man, fearful of his own weakness, has created new and different Gods to whom he might submit; and each time he has surrendered a part of his own power, responsibility, and duty. Gradually, however, men

have become aware that the Gods are his creations, and can
have no power of their own. In moments of exceptional boldness,
Hess continued, men have even challenged the fearsome powers
they have created—witness 1789. Both the prelude to the perfect
society and the final moral revolution will have occurred when
men finally understand that all power, truth, and value belong to
them; from then on, men's actions will not be controlled or determined from outside, nor will they have to be, for man will
know there is nothing to determine him but his own determination.

However brave man might be when driven to oppose God and
King—the deities of his ancestors—he still trembles in anxious
fear before that most powerful God of his own creation—Mam-
mon. This was the theme of two essays on economics Hess wrote
in 1844.[31] Hess could make no contribution to economic theory
as it had been understood since Adam Smith and the French
economists of the eighteenth century, as the science of the nature and social effects of the relationships between the factors
of production and exchange. Hess's philosophy of the omnipotent spirit denied at the outset even the very possibility that "objective relationships between things" could determine or even
limit the actions of men. For Hess, the belief in such a realm of
external law was but evidence of man's spiritual backwardness.
We know now that the limits to man's economic activity are far
more flexible than the Classical Economists assumed, but Hess
would not have been satisfied with just this much; for him, matter and its laws were but images of the spirit, falsely assumed as
independent and powerful by those unaware that man sets his
own limits. Accordingly, Hess acquired no more than a passing
acquaintance with the more popular slogans of those—like John
Prince-Smith in Germany—who presented the conclusions of the
Ricardians at second-hand to the German public, and Hess made
no attempt to meet the Classical Economists on their own
ground.

The struggle for private gain in competitive society and the
economic theories which justify that struggle, Hess insisted, are
at once new proofs of man's fear of responsibility and the last

obstacles to social reform. That same dualistic consciousness which had plagued man throughout the Christian era—the belief that the ideal and the real belong to separate realms of human experience—Hess continued, has sanctioned the brute terror of competitive society. Economists and theologians together have created a "world of body without spirit, and a world of spirit without body." [32] In the Ricardian's defense of selfishness, Hess found the modern expression of that fatal dualism which had always sundered the real from the ideal, and at the expense of both. Indeed, had not Christian idealism prepared the world for its opposite, capitalist materialism? Is not the struggle for personal profit in this world the counterpart of the struggle for personal salvation in the next? The private God of the Protestants and the private property of the bourgeoisie, Hess wrote, do they not belong together? Not only has Christianity outlived its usefulness, it has become one of the chief obstacles to those who would make society divine, for it has upheld a view of the world which compels man to accept voluntarily the ruthless egotism of the war of all against all in industrial society, where each "must sell himself, rent himself, make a thing of himself, or starve." [33] And under "free" enterprise, man has been emptied of all spiritual content, he has become a commodity. "Egoism has come full cycle, and it has attained its most perfect expression in free enterprise society. . . . Here man is at once thief, murderer, slave, deceiver, usurer, worker and beggar." [34]

Once man has stripped all deities of their power, Hess continued, it is only natural that he become the most brutal egoist. For this reason and in spite of its terrors, is not competitive free enterprise the first sign of the liberation of man? To "prove" this Hess again invoked the dialectical method, according to which an idea, once it has attained complete expression, must be replaced by its opposite. Hence the next and final stage of world-history, Hess concluded, will be one in which the individual will submit his will to the will of the community. (Fichte had used the dialectical method to say the same thing forty years earlier.) But Hess was not allowed to extricate himself so easily from the problem of the general will versus the freedom of the individual. Max Stirner, a follower of Feuerbach and a left-Hegelian, was quick to denounce this notion. Have we, he asked, banished God and King only to humble ourselves before another abstraction, the community? To ask man to sacrifice himself to anything, including the *Guetergemeinschaft*, is a sham and an excuse for new tyranny.

> To me, the egoist, the 'well-being' of human society means nothing. I sacrifice nothing to it, I only exploit it, and to exploit it thoroughly I transform it into my property and my creature; that is, I destroy it and put in its place an association of egoists.[35]

In answer to Stirner's criticism and as a reply to the theories of individualism gaining popularity among the left-Hegelians and supported by Stirner and Bruno Bauer, Hess presented the most important doctrine of his true socialism. "The essence of man . . . is his social essence, that is, the cooperation of different individuals for one and the same purpose, and for completely identical interests." [36] By nature, he argued, man is not an egoist, but a socialist; he does not want to conflict with his fellows, but cooperate with them. Why then, it might be argued, has man not acted according to this "essence" in the past? Because, Hess replied, only the free acts of a being reveal its essence, and man has not acted freely in the past because he believed himself subject to various outside forces, the state, religion, and now, the laws of economics. And it is wrong to judge man's nature from his past performance, for: "In the course of history, the essence of man develops itself . . . through struggles and disturbances." [37] Like all things, man develops in time, and it is as wrong to judge man's nature by past history as it would be to judge the flower by the seed.

Using an idea which Marx was later to find of great value, Hess declared further that the social or cooperative nature of man was enhanced by the cooperation in work and commerce found in advanced industrial societies. In this way, he continued, man's nature has been both expressed and stimulated by the productive powers released under capitalism. "The organic community, the ripe fruit of human development, could not come to life as long as we were not entirely developed, and we could not develop ourselves if we did not come into commerce with one another." [38] Thus, and in general outline, the path of history seemed the same to Hess as it had seemed to many utopian Socialists: first the war of all against all, when man was in the brute state of nature; then the beginnings of commerce, industry, and social cooperation; and finally, in industrial society, the contradiction between selfishness and cooperation raised to its highest and final pitch, with full cooperation in production and ruthless egoism in distribution, and the whole being sanctified by the Classical Economists. But the end is not yet, and history has been the education of the human race.

> For through this struggle we have gained something totally different from that for which we fought and hoped. We believed we were winning external goods but we have really developed ourselves. This misconception, however, was helpful and stimulating only so long as it really furthered the increase of our powers and abilities. Once those have been developed, we can only destroy ourselves if we do not make the transition to communism. [39]

Expressing again a notion which Marx was to take up and make the dominant theme of scientific socialism, Hess insisted that under the capitalist mode of production the productivity of man and his well-being cannot be increased any further. For Hess also, capitalism was a necessary stage of history. But the progressive misery of the proletariat, and the desperate search for markets abroad while millions starve at home, demonstrate, Hess insisted, that free enterprise has placed fetters on the development of man toward freedom. [40] Unlike Marx, however, Hess did not believe that socialism must be the next stage of history because the social relationships of industrial society hinder the development of the mode of production, but because these relationships are abhorrent to the moral awareness of men. That is the great contradiction which will impel men toward a communal society.

> This petty world of shopkeepers is a sham and a lie. Under
> the appearance of absolute independence, absolute need; un-
> der the appearance of the most lively trade, the most deadly
> isolation of each from his fellow man; under the appearance of
> an assured and inviolate private property for all, all true prop-
> erty taken from man; and under the appearance of the most
> general freedom, the most general bondage. Is it any wonder,
> then, that in this world of lies, deceit is the norm, honesty an
> insult, bootlicking succeeds to all honors, the honest man falls
> victim to misery and shame, hypocrisy celebrates her triumph,
> truth is regarded as impolite . . . the freest insight is the most
> 'destructive,' and the most extreme servility is the most 'con-
> structive.' [41]

Hess could do little to satisfy those curious as to the details of
the future society; an anarchist, as I have said before, has no laws
and institutions to describe. Furthermore, one who believes that
with socialism man will for the first time consciously set out to
create a perfect society is not likely to presume on man's future
capabilities by prediction. Accordingly, Hess confined himself to
a few hints dropped here and there while discussing related topics. In the society of the future, "production and consumption . . .
work and pleasure," will not be separated, for each will work at
the task best suited to his abilities, will be rewarded correspondingly, and will find his pleasure in his work.[42] For, Hess asked, is
not virtue self-directed and self-stimulated activity, and hence
truly its own reward? And is not vice activity done from fear and
external compulsion?[43] Fourier's influence is obvious. Had not
Fourier argued that the perfect society would be created because
God could not have given man passions and hopes which His
other creations could not fulfill? Similarly, but starting with the
omnipotent creative spirit of man, Hess argued that the virtuous
society would be one in which man's ideals would find full expression without the need of that external law which is necessary
for the imperfect and the unfulfilled.

It follows that a social anarchist who places his faith in the moral evolution of mankind can have no program for revolution. The perfect society will come when the majority of men desire it; then a revolution will be unnecessary, before then it would be folly. Nor will there be a rule of force once the transition has begun, property will not be expropriated, and God and the state will not be abolished by decree: a minority will not need to use force to abolish that which the moral consciousness of the majority has already rejected. There may be, Hess indicated, a brief period when national workshops will be established to relieve the misery of the unemployed, but they will soon give way to voluntarily formed "work-circles." [44] All these arrangements will be decided by men whose moral consciousness has ended the barbaric need of force and compulsion.

To those who objected that man was too corrupt for such a society, Hess replied that man as he is now cannot be used as a standard by which to judge man as he will be when his moral evolution has been completed.

If all men are educated according to human principles, if, further, the special abilities of each are developed and if, finally, each is offered the means with which to practice his abilities, then human society will be organized according to the laws of her nature, then society will be a living body in which all the parts are fully formed and organically one with the whole, and perform their function without need or force, out of an inner, vital force. [45]

For Hess and all Utopians, education and self-development formed the most effective revolutionary strategy, moral persuasion the most successful tactics. Eighteen forty-five was the year when Hess's radical idealism reached its height; then he believed the perfect society possible because it was a possibility of thought. In a universe where the only power is thought man can go wherever the spirit moves him. "Already we can see in the distance the praised land of the future, already we can reach with our eyes the promised land toward which all the previous history of mankind has pointed." [46]

Between Utopianism and Scientism:
Moses Hess, 1846-1875

Most German radicals began to turn from idealism to different varieties of "tough-mindedness" after the disappointments of the post-revolutionary years. Moses Hess, we know, experienced a similar change; but his turn to "realism" started in 1846 and ended with his conversion to scientific socialism as then conceived by Karl Marx. For through his attempts to propagate his ideas in journals and before meetings of workers, Hess had gained a foretaste of the reaction from the censors and police agents of Prussia and the German *Bund*. More important, perhaps, Hess came directly under the influence of Karl Marx. From 1846 on Hess collaborated with both Marx and Engels and increasingly found his own utopionism challenged by Marx in letter and conversation. Indeed, Hess shared in that process by which Marx abstracted all the "tough" ideas from previous socialist theory and caused them to stand alone and forbidding, fit weapons for a later generation of cynical idealists searching desperately to destroy those who had brought them to despair of the power of ideas and ethics.

Hess had known both Marx and Engels since the Berlin days

of the left-Hegelians in 1841, and all three were aware of one another's work during the forties. And when Marx first began to expound the principles of scientific socialism, he could already regard Hess as his first convert from the ranks of the Utopians. Indeed, at the very time when Marx was at work on Engels' first draft of the *Communist Manifesto,* Hess, Engels, and Marx were all working for the *Deutsch-Bruesseler Zeitung;* it was for this paper that Hess—in October and November of 1847—began a series of articles which demonstrated his conversion from utopianism to most of the principles Marx was to reveal a few months later in the *Manifesto.*[1] When Marx and Engels began to denounce true socialism they were well aware that Hess had repudiated his past, but even so they could not trust him.[2] They never really believed he had lost his idealism and utopianism, and events were to prove them correct. For during the revolutions of 1848, Hess's utopian attitude reasserted itself, and from then dates the extreme hostility of Marx and Engels toward Hess.

Before Marx and Engels had cast off their own utopianism of the mid-forties, however, they shared a high regard for Hess. In 1844, Marx named Hess and Engels as the two leading German Socialists, and this was the Hess of the omnipotent and creative moral ego, and of the philosophy of the act.[3] Moreover, in March of 1845, Engels, Marx, and Hess planned to collaborate and publish a series of translations of French and English Socialists, with appropriate introductions.[4] Even then, however, Engels mildly reproved Hess's tendency to underrate the value of empiricism and materialism.[5] Nevertheless, one fact not generally known should be stressed: Hess wrote one brief section of *The German Ideology,* the very work, that is to say, which has been hailed as the first great landmark of scientific socialism and which was, in part, designed as an attack on German true socialism.[6] The attack on utopianism was begun by all three during 1845 and 1846, and in so doing, all three were repudiating some part of their past allegiance to the "German ideology."

This collaboration and Hess's conversion may explain why it was that when Marx and Engels attacked true socialism before

1848, they did not denounce Hess, the leader of that group, but
only his followers.[7] In January of 1845, Engels wrote to Marx:
"The latest is that Hess and I starting on the first of April . . .
will edit a monthly journal, the *Gesellschaftsspiegel* and in it will
describe the misery of society and the rule of the bourgeoisie."[8]
Hess, the Editor in Chief, did not intend the *Gesellschaftsspiegel*
to be just another organ for discussing philosophy and history in
the left-Hegelian manner. Instead, and as he indicated in the
subtitle, it was to be "An organ to represent the unpropertied
classes and to throw light on the social circumstances of the present." Accordingly, Hess described the miserable working conditions of the railroad workers, factory hands, and domestic serv-
ants; Engels wrote of the proletariat of other lands; and articles
on starvation, alcoholism, and prostitution among the working
classes were included. To supplement the journal's effect, Hess
and Engels, in February 1845, held public meetings in a *Gasthof*
in Elberfeld and invited the citizenry to hear readings from Shel-
ley and to consider the abolition of private property.[9] The meetings were a great success, and whatever Engels was to think
later of the efficacy of moral persuasion, in 1845 he was enthusiastic. As Engels wrote to Marx:

> The thing [meetings] attracts tremendously. One speaks of
> nothing here but communism, and every day we gain new
> supporters. There is truly communism in the Wuppertal, it is
> nearly a force. You cannot imagine how favorable the ground
> here is.[10]

But it did not last. The police also attended the meetings. A
threat to the landlady sufficed, and the gatherings were canceled.
As for the *Gesellschaftsspiegel*, after twelve issues Hess had to
stop publication and head for the border, Engels having preceded
him. Once more the agents of reaction had done their best to
further the transition from utopianism to scientism, and soon
Marx would provide the means to do battle against such "objective conditions of existence" as censorship and oppression. Correspondingly, Hess's work on the journal forced him to reconsider

his belief in the omnipotence of pure spirit, for when he described the life of the workers under capitalism, their very misery gave him pause. Perhaps there were, after all, forces even more powerful than man's moral self-awareness holding back the realization of socialism. Along with Marx and Engels, Hess turned his attention to the laws of economics and the material conditions of capitalist society. For however brief a time, the most radical Utopian of them all turned scientist.

It is true, as Zlocisti maintained, that the beginnings of the new attitude towards socialism can be traced in some of Hess's writings from 1845 through 1846. For example, when discussing the failure of a group of "bourgeois" Socialists in a canton in Switzerland, men who, after gaining office, failed to carry their principles into practice, Hess remarked: "Only the proletariat can make a thoroughgoing break with present conditions." [11] The rest of the essay shows, however, that it was anger Hess expressed rather than new theoretical principles. Marx was more fit by taste and temperament for purges—both political and intellectual—and it was under Marx's influence that Hess became, in 1847, one of the first three scientific Socialists.

Hess, as we saw, always insisted on Marx's supremacy in matters of theory, but he never respected Marx's party tactics. When Marx insulted Weitling and drove the German Utopians, Schapper and Willich, out of the workers' organization in London, Hess came to their defense. Was it really in the interests of socialism to split the handful of German radicals into opposing camps, thus making them even more ineffective against the common enemy? As Hess wrote to Marx: "With you personally I should like to have a great deal to do, with your party, however, I will have nothing to do." [12] And can it not be argued that the insistence on doctrinal purity which Marx left as a legacy to his followers did as much to hold up the cause of social reform as Marx's theories did to advance it? Were not the most effective Socialists always Utopians at heart, however abjectly they humbled themselves before the structure of the great dialectical materialist? But the chief of the two-man "International Workers' Organization in

London" would have greeted the accusation with scorn. How could any action of his weaken a party already helpless because its leaders preached class cooperation in an age of class struggle? Far better to have no party at all. And once Hess had accepted Marx's theories, he had no effective reply. One cannot reject Marx's tactics without casting aside his ideology as well—they are of a piece.

As Hess's later work shows, he was a scientific Socialist in theory but Utopian at heart, ever unable to choose one and exclude the other. As far as theory is concerned, Hess signified his capitulation in a letter to Marx on July 28, 1846.

> With your views as to communist writings . . . I agree fully. Necessary as it was in the beginning to tie communistic efforts to the German ideology [philosophical idealism], so it is now just as necessary to base them on historical and economic assumptions, otherwise we will never be finished with the "Socialists" or with the opponents of all colors. Now I also have thrown myself exclusively into economic literature, and await with suspense the appearance of your work, which I shall study with great diligence.[13]

As Hess's letter indicates, Marx thought true socialism justifiable in the early forties because neither the laws of capitalist economics nor the class struggle were evident then in Germany. But since then, Marx argued, the laws and the struggle have been revealed, and it is nonsense to continue to find one's inspiration in the outmoded moral categories of German philosophical idealism. Those who did so were denounced by him and Engels in *The German Ideology,* Hess alone excepted. In *From Hegel to Marx,* Sidney Hook has shown Marx's objection to true socialism to have been primarily tactical; those who place their faith in abstract (or classless) morality and in the essence of man (again regardless of class) give comfort to the reactionaries by denying the force of the class struggle and the need for revolution.[14] Only the proletariat, Marx continued, have the moral awareness needed for communism, because their material existence contradicts their human needs. In a quotation well chosen, Marx's condemnation of true socialism is made clear.

> In the real world there exists, on the one side, owners of private property and on the other, a propertyless communist proletariat. This opposition becomes sharper day by day and is heading for a crisis. Consequently, if the theoretical representatives of the proletariat desire to accomplish anything by their literary activity, they must above all get rid of all phrases which weaken the intensity of this opposition, all phrases which glide over the opposition and which offer the bourgeoisie an opportunity, impelled by its sentimental quest for security, to approach the proletariat. All of these bad characteristics we find in the slogans of the true Socialists . . . we are well aware that the communist movement cannot be corrupted by a pair of German phrase-mongers. But it is necessary in a country like Germany where philosophical phrases have for centuries had a certain power, and where the absence of the sharp class oppositions which prevail among other nations makes the communist consciousness less militant and decisive, to oppose all phrase-making which waters down and weakens still further the consciousness of the total opposition of communism to the existing world order.[15]

Of course, Marx made no Sorelian distinction between truth and tactics; and Hess came to accept the Marxist premises which are inseparable from the tactical appeal.[16]

The reversal was striking and complete. Three years earlier Hess had sacrificed the material world to the omnipotent pure spirit; in 1847, he proclaimed that ideas are but "the theoretical expression . . . of material facts," and he denounced with Marx those "German Ideologists" who still believed in the primacy and power of "eternal truths."

> What is it that characterizes the Ideologists? It is their faith in ideas and in the immortality and autonomy of 'absolute truth.' But truth is always the truth of a situation, the true expression of the conditions through which a situation exists. Without these conditions the truth would contradict itself, negate and destroy itself, and consequently would not exist at

all—yet in the fancy of the Ideologists, truth is something that has no relationship to material conditions and relates to itself alone.[17]

Blinded by this confusion between idea and reality, Hess continued, the Ideologists accept the ruling ideas of the day—the ideas, that is to say, of the ruling classes—and ennoble them as absolute truths. In this manner, the Ideologists sanction the exploitation of the proletariat characteristic of free enterprise. Denouncing, in effect, his own activities since 1836, Hess wrote: ". . . the people will no longer let themselves be put off with ideas and principles, or with beautiful sounding oratory about brotherly love, freedom, and equality. . . ."[18]

If the spirit is but a reflex of matter and if man's social values are determined by his material conditions of existence, then Hess had to discard his earlier faith in the power of man's communal nature and man's moral awareness of that nature. And once spirit has been deprived of its autonomy, there can be no dialectical give and take between spirit and matter. Also discarded, then, was Hess's admiration for German philosophical idealism. Like Marx, he kept the terminology but lost the vision which had informed it. Hess no longer regarded himself as the mediator between the sundered halves of the World-Spirit—German speculation and French activism—for Hess, German idealism was no longer a revolutionary force. With Marx he turned to the west; there the laws of economics and the class struggle consequent upon industrialization stood stark and powerful, and from there, hence, the revolution must come to Germany.

> . . . the German bourgeoisie appears damned to veer between fear and hope, becalmed on the still ocean of German misery, until the great storm from the west breaks loose, and the waves of the proletariat, frothing up out of the depths, smash away King, nobility and bourgeoisie. Let us leave the German bourgeoisie and the German misery to their fate, and direct our view to that approaching storm and its consequences.[19]

In 1847, Marx, Engels, and Hess became preoccupied with the

laws of economics as revealed by the Classical Economists and presented by the utopian Socialists. What separated these three Socialists at the time from the utopian Socialists, however, was not that old preoccupation but a new dependence. In 1847 and '48, they added nothing new to the old arguments from economic law, but they did make them the main arguments. If that is not original, it is at least revolutionary. As a consequence, we find the paradox of Socialists urging on the very egoism of free enterprise that it was their hope to curb! For, as Hess wrote in "Die Folgen der Revolution des Proletariats," the results of the search for private gain will be the inevitable collapse of capitalism, brought down by the tension of its economic contradictions.[20] By driving out their less efficient competitors, capitalists will raise productivity to the maximum, and will also concentrate all wealth in the hands of a few. The oversupply of labor will assure that its price, like the price of all commodities, will decrease to the minimum, the cost of its reproduction or the subsistence level. Consequently, laborers will not be able to buy the very goods they produce, and the results of this crisis through "overproduction" will be unemployment, hunger, desperation and revolution.

This is the common and far-too-simple analysis which was incorporated before Hess into the tradition of utopian socialism. (It is well known that Sismondi and Rodbertus had achieved a far more sophisticated knowledge of the theory and practice of capitalism long before 1848.) Hess's study of economics had evidently not gone beyond an acquaintance with these staples of the utopian criticism of capitalism, and, unlike Marx, he was to do no independent work in economic theory. For Hess, the rigid simplicities of this deductive order replaced his earlier faith in the moral creativity of man. If the capitalists could not be persuaded by the plain justice of the workers' demands, no matter— they would be destroyed by the workings of the laws of capitalism. Hess had found irresistible forces independent of the frail uncertainties of moral persuasion.

Still, even this scheme, like that of the *Communist Manifesto*, does not depend upon the laws of objective forces but on the blind rapacity and supreme selfishness of the bourgeoisie. If the capitalists do not take all surplus value, and if they do not strive to keep wages down to the subsistence minimum, none of the "laws" will work and revolution will not be the inevitable prelude to reform. No amount of economic analysis can obscure this essential fact: the question of social reform is a moral question, and the scientific Socialists postulated a certain kind of moral world order as surely as had the Utopians. As Sorel clearly saw, none of the "iron" laws will work unless the capitalists commit themselves to exclusive class domination of the most oppressive sort. For Hess, Marx, and Engels in 1847, however, the claim of objectivity was a reflex of pessimism and an expression of their desire for a kind of certainty which the older optimism could no longer provide.

With the same thought that occurred to Marx and Engels earlier, that the social revolution will come where industrialism has advanced the furthest, Hess looked to England. As a result of increasing imbalance between production and consumption there will be one last crisis, Hess wrote; bills of exchange will no longer be honored at London, goods will not move, masses of unemployed will haunt the streets of the capitals of the world, and international capitalism will collapse in ruins.

> A great world conflagration will begin against which the uniformed minions of the palace owners will be helpless, because it will break out everywhere and at the same time . . . everywhere the people will seize political power and put the idle instruments of production back to work on behalf of the state. Everywhere men will follow the example of the English proletariat and work will be organized. Out of the ruins of private industry a new and splendid world industry will arise, one which will not be run for the profit of individual owners of private property, to the great misfortune of the working class, but will be run communally and in the interests of all the people.[21]

After the revolution, Hess continued, all privately owned industrial property will be nationalized, worker's councils will manage the economy, inheritance laws and a progressive tax will expropriate the expropriators, the state will guarantee work, and there will be free education for all.

As with so many German social theorists who originally found their inspiration in the work of the philosophical Idealists, Hess had to find a world-view within which to fit his new ideas as to the particulars of socialist theory. He followed Marx and became a materialist. During 1850, Hess corresponded with Alexander Herzen and asked him to read Marx if he wished to see the weaknesses of the Idealists exposed by one who had the true, "realistic," and "materialistic" conception of the world and history.[22] To paraphrase a passage from one of Hess's letters to Herzen: if one does not understand that morals and religion are but the reflex of objective social conditions which are themselves created by the dominant "mode of production," one turns the world upside down, and mistakes the apex of social reality for the base.[23] Not only did Hess reject his idealism of the forties, he, like so many of those disillusioned by the reaction of the fifties, turned in desperation to the study of the "real facts," the ultimate realities as revealed by the sciences of matter. Here he thought he would find a source of truth with which to replace the speculative excesses of German philosophy.

In a series of articles and book reviews written for French and German periodicals during the fifties, Hess announced his conversion to materialism, and, like so many German intellectuals of the day, gave to Vogt and Moleschott (the leaders of the materialistic opponents of idealism) the allegiance he had once given to Fichte and Hegel. In an article entitled the "Natural Sciences and Social Theory," he argued against those who still believed in the absolute and independent nature of moral judgments.[24] An individual's moral judgments, he insisted, are determined by his position in society; these social relationships are in turn determined by the mode of production; and, finally, the mode of production is itself changed by advances made in the exact sciences that are utilized in technology.[25] The service rendered by Marx, that of basing socialism on the laws of economics, he continued, has made socialism itself one of the exact sciences and as such independent of mere enthusiasm.[26] Materialism is the only possible basis for morality today, and a belief in the power of "idealistic morality is now but a pious wish, if not worse." [27] Hess praised Marx and Moleschott as twin leaders of a new generation which had found more wisdom in exact science than had been contained in all the theological mumblings about the "Absolute" presented by a generation of speculative mystics. For a time Hess even refused to employ the older philosophic terminology, for it "reminds one too much of the old illusions." [28]

Hess had forsaken the Absolute, pure Spirit, and dialectical idealism, and he retained only the formal outline of the German Idealists' view of history. Only now, instead of the supremacy of mind and the march of increasing moral self-awareness through history, Hess found in economic determinism and the advance of technology the means for comprehending world-history. He had lost the old vision but had not discarded the corresponding habit: that of searching for sweeping and all-inclusive generalizations. Embarking, in the fifties, on a journey through the literature of astronomy, physics, chemistry and economics, Hess prepared himself for the discovery of an all-inclusive theory capable of explaining the development of the cosmos, organic life, and society. He was not the only one to yield to this impulse; Comte was doing the same in France. And in all this science there was still much utopianism!

No matter how much Hess desired to join the ranks of the "scientists," he could not do more than temporarily still his utopian impulses. For in spite of his high regard for theory, Hess was extraordinarily sensitive to experience. And whenever experience seemed to offer hope, Hess returned to his utopian attitude. Two experiences especially caused his old attitude to revive —the revolutions of 1848 and the career of the brilliant and always Utopian founder of modern German socialism, Ferdinand Lassalle.

The "mad years" of revolution tore the thin veneer of scientism from the old Utopian. As Kings fell and barricades arose, Hess found it unrealistic to remain a realist. He was outraged by Marx's strictures against those who believed they could turn the revolutions into immediate victories for socialism and the proletariat. German radicals were pouring back into Germany, a revolutionary legion was formed and the red banner was seen flying once again over the domains of the Hohenzollerns. For all this, Marx had nothing but scorn. Economic conditions, Marx argued, are not ripe enough for the proletarian revolution; to gain anything the workers must cooperate with the bourgeoisie. Hess's revived utopianism drew his allegiance temporarily away from Marxism; during 1849 he sympathized with the more radical Socialists. An open letter attacking Marx but not written by Hess expressed well this more extreme position.

> Must we really, Herr Preacher, as you advise us, avoid the inferno of the Middle Ages by throwing ourselves into the purgatory of the decrepit rule of capital, so that from there we may gain the misty paradise of your Communist articles of faith? *[Glaubensbekenntnis]*

How can you or anyone else, the author exclaimed, write the history of the future? Men's acts, not your laws of economics, will determine what is to be.

> You are not really interested in the freedom of the oppressed. For you the misery of the workers and the hunger of the poor are only of scientific and doctrinal interest. You are above such miseries. . . . You are not gripped by that which moves the hearts of men. You do not believe in the cause you pretend to represent. Yes, in spite of the fact that every day you cut the German Revolution according to the stencil of completed fact, yes, in spite of your *Communist Manifesto [Glaubensbekenntnis]*, you do not believe in the revolution of the workers, whose climbing floods have already prepared the downfall of capital; you do not believe in the permanence of the revolution, you do not even believe in your own revolutionary capabilities.

Bitterness and anger gripped the unknown author as he thought of his own conversion to scientific socialism; evidently Hess was not the only Utopian converted by Marx before 1848!

> If only you had not gone through this great change, if only we had not let your phrases confuse us . . . then we ourselves would not have to do penance today for believing you when you made the revolution in Germany depend on the revolution of the French petty-bourgeoisie, and the revolution of the proletariat in France depend on the revolution of the proletariat in England, and when you made the victory of the proletarian revolution *ueberhaupt*, depend upon the development of industry and the rule of the bourgeoisie—things which one could only wait for.[29]

As President of the German Workers League in Paris, Hess had done what he could with his pen to aid the revolutions. In 1849 he fled to Switzerland as the agents of Prussia and France began rounding up the left.[30] In Geneva and Zurich, Hess shared his despair with the wretched colonies of pursued revolutionists. Because they could not come to grips with their true enemies, these dispossessed fought among themselves. Theories, manifestos, proclamations, and prophecies multiplied; theoretical differences were often settled with sword or pistol. Many, weary of Europe, left for good—these were the years when the *Amerika-Tollwut* reached its height. Hess did not join them. In spite of all the disappointments he had suffered, and even though he never challenged Marx's supremacy as an economic theorist, he was not willing to wait for "conditions" to become "ripe"; Lenin would have admired him.

In London, the other camp for displaced revolutionists, Schapper and Willich, still Utopians and hoping to continue the revolution, broke with Marx and took the majority with them. They differed as to the timing of the revolution. As Zlocisti put it: "The radicals wanted to strike immediately. Tomorrow. Marx wanted to wait until the necessary economic crisis followed the momentary boom. The day after tomorrow." [31] Hess became secretary of the organization started by Schapper and Willich, and, provided with a forged passport, left for Germany in 1852. Wanted for high treason, he had to leave Germany, and until the summer of 1854 he wandered from city to city, through Germany, Belgium, and Holland, finally finding respite in his adopted homeland, France. There he took up once more his work in the natural sciences.

In 1851, Hess had written of Marx and Engels: "They understand excellently the art of dissecting the body of our society, and know how to expose its economy and its sickness. But they are too materialistic to possess that spirit which electrifies and transports the people." [32] Working in London, Marx and Engels were necessarily out of touch with attempts to organize the workers on the continent, and this as well as their violent atacks on all Utopians caused Hess to remain away from their London group, concentrate on his own studies, and do what he could to maintain connections with the scattered and ineffective radical organizations of Europe.

In 1863, however, his work was interrupted by one more chance for political action, and Hess could not refuse. Ferdinand Lassalle, still a Forty-eighter, had stimulated and transformed the German Workingmens' Association into the first socialist organization in Germany since the reaction, and he wanted Hess to represent him in the Rhineland. In letters to Hess, Lassalle asked him not to let theoretical differences prevent his helping to organize the German workers so that they might better press their claims against the state and the liberals of the Progressive party.[33] Lassalle need not have worried; Hess's admiration for the economic theories of Karl Marx never drove him to deny the power of will and action to create the conditions necessary for socialism. With Lassalle, Hess believed that the constitutional crisis of the early sixties offered an excellent opportunity to form the workers of Germany into an independent political force. By June of 1863, he was back in Cologne.

Theory, jealousy, and, perhaps, the quietism of despair caused Marx to look with scorn on the rebirth of German socialism.

So Lassalle collects those who were excreted from our party twenty years ago for his dung factory, with which world his-

tory shall be manured. So he has named Moses Hess as his
viceroy in the Rhine province. Oh youth, oh youth, what were
you thinking of when you let yourself be hanged on Herwegh
and Moses Hess! [34]

Repeatedly, and on the grounds that the masses of Germany did
not yet desire socialism, Marx and Engels castigated Lassalle's attempts to gain "general and direct" votes for the people. Of course
Lassalle and Hess were quite aware of the apathy of the masses,
but they thought it the task of Socialists to create the desire for
social reform and to assure that desire political voice; they saw
that nothing would be lost if they tried to do both at once. To
the objections from London, Hess answered:

> According to the Marxist recipe of 1847, the workers should
> not press their claims against the bourgeoisie, and, in fact,
> should work with them, until the bourgeoisie has gained its
> own demands, for by this means the ground will have been
> prepared on which the workers can carry on their own battle
> with the bourgeoisie. This general and, as a matter of historical
> fact, long employed revolutionary strategy is certainly obvious
> and did not need to be presented as new dogma in 1847, nor
> does it need repeating now. Less understandable, however,
> are the conclusions that the reader is supposed to deduce from
> all this. Because the final demands of the bourgeoisie have not
> been achieved anywhere in Europe, Lassalle's organization is
> too early; one must wait until the Republic is once again de-
> clared and a 'Neueste Rheinische Zeitung' can be started. Un-
> til then one should fold one's arms and with dumb devotion
> look to Mecca-London. [35]

Hess's new view of socialism—one he was to maintain until his
death in 1875—was a reaffirmation of his original utopian insistence on the power of will, stripped of his earlier theological and
phenomenological pretensions, however, by a new awareness of
the limitations placed on man's aspirations by given circumstances, and governed by his new desire not to presume too much
on immediate possibilities. In his first speech to members of Lassalle's organization in the Rhineland, he emphasized the power

of will and presented proposals which show both the influence of Lassalle and a new respect for the concrete.

> By itself, the general development of industry is not a sufficient explanation for the political-social movement of contemporary Europe. . . . If it is true that all great political changes have social and economic class contradictions as their basis . . . it is, nevertheless, also true that only activistic nations—like the French in modern times and the Romans in ancient times—are able to transform these class contradictions into a class struggle, and so bring the mightiest element in society to political rule.[36]

How else, he asked, can we explain the apparent paradox presented by England, for is not England ahead of France industrially and yet far behind in radicalism and revolution? Doubtless, he continued, the general cause of the Revolution of February was the state of industry, but certainly its specific cause "lay in the peculiar character of the French nation." [37] And in Germany the same economic contradictions exist, but the German worker is not yet aware of the conflict between his demands and those of the bourgeoisie, while the bourgeoisie itself has not yet had the courage to overthrow the feudal aristocracy which still decides the fate of the Germanies! In Germany, material conditions are not simply ripe, they are overripe; it is a question then of moral persuasion and propaganda. Consciousness and desire are all, and if they are not created in Germany, misery and exploitation will go on forever. The "creative spirit of the people" awoke, Hess continued, and made its demands known in 1789 and 1848 in France, and it is the task of Lassalle's organization to stimulate that same spirit in Germany.

For one who believes in the primacy of will over material conditions, the laws of economics are no longer the chief topics of interest; this is one reason why, after his brief excursion into economic theory in 1846 and 1847, Hess did no more independent work in that field. And when Hess, his utopianism revived in 1863, pointed out the economic contradictions of capitalism, he did not regard them as the motive force behind social reform, but as conditions making for the desirability of social reform. Furthermore, Hess no longer adhered to those laws of economics which, following Marx, he had selected in 1847 from the rich variety of the socialist tradition. We know now, he told the workers of the Rhineland, that the worker's real wages have increased, not decreased since the beginning of the Industrial Revolution. Because he no longer believed in one of the prime articles of Marxist faith—the iron law of wages—Hess could view capitalism with a new sense of the possibility for reform without crisis and bloody revolution, and he no longer needed to look for anything like the drastic changes he had thought necessary throughout the forties. He was no longer motivated by his anarchistic unwillingness to accept anything short of paradise, or by his "scientific" conviction that the largest class of society was doomed to ever-increasing misery.

Still, Hess continued, we cannot expect the real wages of the workers to continue increasing, because the system of production and exchange that came in with the Industrial Revolution was not responsible for these increases in the first place. Rather, Hess argued, such increases were caused by the great technological achievements and discoveries which accompanied the Industrial Revolution. All the basic discoveries have been made, Hess continued rather arbitrarily, and we can no longer count on such great increases in the wealth of society. Consequently, the system by which the distribution of wealth is carried on must itself be changed, and that can be done—perhaps Hess had been reading John Stuart Mill—without changing greatly the mode of production. Pointing to another problem that had concerned Mill, Hess argued that distribution must be changed so that the consuming power of the workers may be greatly increased. As things are now, he wrote, the capitalists gain all "surplus value," and therefore are unable to dispose of their products at home. With the consequent search for new markets abroad goes the ever more damaging cycle of boom and bust. Moreover, the situation is made worse by the general unplanned nature of capitalist production and distribution. Capitalists do not produce to meet the demands of a new market, they produce for profit. Accordingly, when a potential market is discovered, those capitalists who can engage in a free-for-all orgy of production in order to capture the whole market, and the result is necessarily, and again, "overproduction," crisis, and depression. From this it follows, Hess concluded, that some means must be found by which surplus value can be taken from the idle coupon clippers and returned to the workers, and the general system of distribution of wealth must be planned. With Lassalle, Hess turned to the state.[38]

Unlike most of the ex-Forty-eighters, Lassalle had not lost hope in the ability of the state to lead in the radical reconstruction of society; Feuerbach's antagonism against the value and efficacy of all such Hegelian "general categories" as the state had not affected Lassalle. Accordingly Lassalle remained an Hegelian of the middle, and agreed that the state might well be the representative of the "Moral Idea" on earth. Lassalle cannot be called naive, for he understood quite well that the state was the result of brute social forces, or classes, and not the result of parliamentary debates about the just political order. As far as Germany was concerned Lassalle's perception of those forces was far more accurate than the simple declarations of the *Communist Manifesto*, declarations which applied not at all to the Germany of Bismarck and Wilhelm but to the France of Louis-Philippe. The throne, the army, the landowning aristocracy, and the most powerful members of the upper bourgeoisie—these, Lassalle correctly saw, were the "social forces" that controlled Germany.[39] Furthermore, it was neither naiveté nor treason against socialism (as Marx and Engels charged) to attempt to add the workers of Germany, through universal suffrage, to that powerful constellation. Bismarck and the conservatives were in need of allies to aid them against the liberal bourgeoisie during the constitutional struggle over the army bill, and Bismarck himself considered the possibility of enlisting the aid of the workers through the vote. Bismarck had, of course, no bourgeois prejudices against using social reform or even universal suffrage to attain his ends.

Certainly if Lassalle and his followers can be said to have

failed in the sixties, it is not because of their excess of hope but because of their lack of time. Less than two years of life remained for Lassalle to carry through his great work. After his death, his followers had but two years more until the roar of cannon at Koeniggraetz, for it was the resurgence of nationalism and the hope of unification which enabled Bismarck to hold together the once shaky coalition of throne, army, and aristocracy. Four years later Sedan completed the evolution; bourgeoisie and masses thought first of Prussia and the nation, and only later of parliament and votes. Even then there were radicals who thought the state could be used to introduce social reform; in fact, whether they confessed it or not, the majority of the Social Democrats in Parliament acted on this principle and they remained, after all, the most powerful socialist party in Europe.

And so, in 1863, Hess told the workers of the Rhineland that the state must guarantee the right to work and assure to the producer the product of his labors.[40] To begin with, the state must extend credit at low interest to producers' associations. Here Hess denounced Lassalle's inveterate enemy, Schulze-Delitsch, who had argued that the workers should form producers' associations without state aid. His movement, supported by members of the Progressive party, was gaining momentum in the Rhineland. Is it not absurd, Hess asked, to expect workers to aid themselves within an economic system which guarantees all surplus value to the owners of the means of production? The state must become the owner of industry, and the investor of capital. The managers of state owned enterprises, Hess suggested, might be elected by the workers and approved by the state, or selected by the state and approved by the workers; in either event the state must reserve the right to withdraw credit from unprofitable enterprises. After the amounts necessary for expansion and maintenance have been subtracted, profits must be shared among the producers, consumption power will be thereby increased, and the disastrous detour of surplus value through the pockets of the coupon clippers will come to an end.

Through its planning commissions, the state will supervise investment and accounts, check inventories, calculate effective demand, and gradually extend its control over industry by founding new enterprises until the constant crises caused by the anarchy of an unplanned society having only the increase of private wealth as its goal will end. The beneficial effects of competition will be maintained (this from the former antagonist of competitive egoism!) because the workers' wages will depend upon the efficiency of his enterprise. Prices will be determind by production, reinvestment, and labor costs; the profits of the bourgeoisie will no longer interrupt the free flow of goods on the world market.[41]

Lassalle's influence on Hess is quite obvious; in all this there is little that Lassalle was not saying at the same time. And in other ways Hess's state socialism of the eighteen-sixties owes much to utopianism; one is reminded that European state socialism had its origin in the utopian tradition and owes nothing to its chief antagonists, the Marxists. Still, Hess the utopian anarchist—as well as Hess the scientific Socialist—fade from view as one reads these later essays. Both the extreme vision of hope which informed the one and the anger of despair which informed the other are gone, and in peaceful reform, the gradual socialization of the means of production, and an appeal to the state, Hess found new prospects for the future of socialism. In contrast with his own past Hess had become a moderate, and so he was to remain until the end of his life in 1875.

It is not surprising that this final change of attitude should have come upon Hess in the eighteen-sixties, for then the potential role of the state in economic affairs was revealed. In a pamphlet he wrote in 1869, *La Haut Finance et l'Empire,* Hess pointed out the powerful influence the state was beginning to wield in industry, and in his speeches in Cologne he indicated the great increases of state economic activity under Louis Napoleon.[42] Hess even appealed to Louis Napoleon to undertake social reform; for this—in his own day and ours—Hess's honesty has been questioned, but nothing warrants the accusation.[43] Even when he made his appeal to Louis Napoleon, Hess insisted that socialism

was not compatible with dictatorship.[44] And it was neither cor-
ruption nor stupidity but fact which Hess pointed to when he
mentioned the increasing influence of the state in such semi-pub-
lic enterprises as railroads, banks, utilities, insurance companies,
and munitions works.[45] Nor did Hess need to find all his exam-
ples in France. As he reminded the workers of Cologne in 1863,
their own city fathers had recently contracted with an English
firm to provide the city with light. Had this enterprise been done
by a city-owned corporation the profits could have been used to
the advantages of the citizens of Cologne. Meanwhile, the con-
struction of a new waterworks was planned, and Hess asked the
workers to agitate for public ownership.[46]

Of course, Hess admitted, most of the economic activity of the
state has heretofore been directed towards the immediate profit
of the bourgeoisie, but great possibilities have been shown, and
what might happen when the representatives of the workers sit
in the parliaments of Europe? For state socialism is but the logi-
cal extension of existing tendencies, Hess seemed to think, and a
true *Volksstaat* might be created without recourse to revolution
or swift and sweeping changes.

Hess was now of the opinion that the fiery radicalism of both
the Utopians and the scientific Socialists was unnecessary. He
began to prefer the word *Volksstaat* to indicate the society of the
future, rather than socialism. Even though all classes (except the
finance capitalists) would benefit from the state ownership and
management of production, the fear inspired in the bourgeois by
the usual words of radical discourse has been a hindrance to reform. The vision of an imminent red dictatorship, and the utopian
[his word] insistence on a total re-building of society, Hess now
thought, have hurt the cause of social reform by blinding the
middle classes to their stake in the new society.[47] There is no
need for bloody revolution, nor for the dictatorship of the proletariat; universal suffrage, moral persuasion, the appeal to interest, and the gradual extension of state control will do the trick.
For the *Volksstaat* will not be demanded by the proletariat alone.
The misery of the workers is the cause of evils which strike every

class but one with nearly equal force; only the finance capitalists have anything to lose. Once the middle classes have lost their fear of the "red spectre," they will recognize the justice and general benefit of the workers' claims; indeed, they will join the workers in the creation of the *Volksstaat*. Hess's final position is clear: the good society will be created by those who have the hope of the Utopians without their ignorance of the limitations of given circumstances, and by those who have the sense of economic reality possessed by Marx but without his despair of the creative powers of man.

In the Germany of 1863, however, the chances of the *Volksstaat* seemed dim. Even Lassalle began to wonder if the workers of Germany could even be roused to agitate for the vote; there were only something over four thousand members of Lassalle's organization just before his tragic death. And it was only six months after he had begun to work for Lassalle that Hess left for Paris. As he wrote to Lassalle in December of 1863:

> As far as I am concerned, I have still the same fanaticism for the social movement that has filled my soul for the last twenty-eight or thirty years . . . but precisely the old age of my fanaticism distinguishes it from yours, for I am not able to make any more illusions for myself. . . . I can [contribute] only if I . . . don't wear out the remainder of my powers in small, so-called practical struggles—struggles which, according to my most inner convictions, will not lead to anything great or decisive—and if I devote myself for a while to theoretical studies and work. . . .[48]

After Lassalle's death Hess wrote a eulogy for him in, appropriately enough, the *Journal des Actionnaires*.[49] And Hess continued to contribute some of his thoughts to those who took up the movement where Lassalle had left it. Throughout the sixties, furthermore, Hess defended Lassallian views before the meetings of the International Workingmen's Association, to which he was often an elected delegate. After 1866, however, Hess withdrew his support from Schweitzer, the leader of the Lassallians, for Hess was convinced, and this time in agreement with Marx, that the Lassallians were more interested in German unity and the rule of Prussia than they were in the freedom and well-being of the workers.[50]

The events of 1870 and 1871 only added to Hess's disgust with the fatherland and his fear for the future of socialism. As an enemy alien, he was forced out of France at the outbreak of the Franco-Prussian war. From Brussels, nevertheless, he wrote a scathing series of anti-Prussian articles.[51] He turned away from Germany for good. France is the land of revolution, freedom, and social progress, Prussia the narrow state of armed reaction; what was this war but another attempt by Prussia to stamp out the flame of freedom first ignited in 1789? His dismay at the victory of Prussia turned to despair as the armies of order wiped out the Commune. Was there no hope left for Europe, the land for whom he had given his life? Finally he returned to Paris. There amidst the ruins, sick and old, he knew that he would never live to see the third era.

Once before, in 1850, fearful of the prospects for socialism, he had turned to natural science in order to find a more secure basis for hope. This he did again in the final years of his life. His last book, the *Dynamische Stofflehre* (published posthumously in 1877) was more than merely another attempt to find in science what he could not find in idealism. Indeed, the goal he set himself reminds one of the vision of unity which had inspired his youth, provided a theme for his first work, and given purpose to his life. He wanted, and thought that he had found, a theory that would "explain all scientific facts," and "condense all the phenomena of the cosmic, organic, and human spheres of life into one strict scientific system. . . ."[52] Undisciplined by empirical considerations, and written by one still hoping to fit all scientific discoveries into one grand metaphysical system, the book makes no contribution to astronomy, physics, or chemistry. It is valuable, however, because it indicates that Hess intended to spend his last years making a synthesis of the two movements which had inspired his life: idealism and materialism.

He planned to devote one volume to each of these three

branches of human knowledge, but he finished only the *Kosmischer Teil*. What he might have had to say about society cannot be known, but he left enough hints in the *Introduction* to reveal the direction of his thought. And he seemed to have worked out a curious compromise between the two tendencies—utopian and scientific—which had been struggling for mastery within him since the dark days of the reaction. Hess began by praising the tendency of the younger generation to base their ideas on empirical investigations.

> After the all-too-great preponderance of philosophical speculation over positive empirical science which prevailed in the first half of the century and especially in Germany, it was natural and, for the progress of human knowledge, desirable that there should be a reaction in favor of the exact sciences. Now it is time, however, not to turn our attention exclusively to philosophical speculation, but to establish a balance between philosophy and empirical science. . . .[53]

All life, he continued—cosmic, organic, and social—is governed by laws which can be empirically known. With the French Revolution began a new power also governed by law: man's consciousness of the laws of politics, economics, and society. Equipped with this awareness, and supported by all the force of the inevitable, man will create the good society. The development of human society toward the realization of man's highest ideals, he wrote, is not only desirable, it is inevitable, for this is in complete accord with the scientific and natural laws which govern social life.

Hess had returned to Spinoza—the *ordo et connexio idearum idem est ac ordo et connexio rerum:* thought and matter are parallel, and neither is supreme because both form the whole. Another theme that Hess presented in his last work shows that the old Utopian still had the upper hand: he insisted that the fundamental reality of the universe was not passive matter, nor even comprehending mind, but warmth, movement, and energy. He had returned to himself.

Notes

Introduction

1. Excellent discussions of Marx's scientism can be found in Jacques Barzun, *Darwin, Marx, Wagner* (Boston, 1941), and John Plamenatz, *German Marxism, Russian Communism* (New York, 1954).
2. See Barzun, *op. cit.*
3. For an example of the traditional unthinking denunciation of utopian socialism, see Franz Mehring, *Geschichte der Deutschen Socialdemokratie* (Stuttgart, 1919), pp. 9-21.
4. Georg Adler, *Rodbertus, der Begruender des wissenschaftlichen Sozialismus* (Leipzig, 1844), pp. 21-60.
5. Plamenatz, *op. cit.*, pp. 164ff.
6. David Riesman, *Individualism Reconsidered* (Glencoe, Illinois, 1954), p. 70. Permission to quote has been granted by *The Free Press*, Chicago, Illinois.

Moses Hess and the Sacred History of Mankind

1. The True Socialists were not a party but an informal group united by allegiance to similar ideas. Next to Hess, Karl Gruen was the most outstanding. Among others the following can be named: Heinrich Puettman, Otto Semmig, Friedrich Schnake, and Georg Herwegh.
2. Letter to Auerbach from Hess, July 19, 1843: *"Wir sprachen ueber die*

Zeitfragen und er [Engels], ein Anno Eins Revolutionaer, schied von mir als allereifrigster Kommunist"; in Hess/Auerbach letters, *Historische Schriften* (New York, 1937), II, 413-43. See also Gustav Mayer, *Friedrich Engels* (The Hague, 1934), I, 103, 117.

3. Theodore Zlocisti, *Moses Hess, der Vorkaempfer des Sozialismus und Zionismus* (Berlin, 1921). With the few exceptions noted below, I am indebted to this excellent biography whenever I speak of Hess's life.

4. Marx and Engels, *Das Kommunistische Manifest* (ninth ed., Berlin, 1930), p. 51.

5. Zlocisti, *op. cit.*, Chapter One.

6. *Ibid.*, p. 20.

7. Zlocisti and Kressel, *Mosheh Hess* (Tel-Aviv, 1947). I do not read Hebrew, and I should like to thank Richard Webster of Columbia University for translating some of these letters for me.

8. Moses Hess, *Die Heilige Geschischte der Menschheit* (Stuttgart, 1837), p. 197.

9. *Ibid.*, p. 211.

10. *Ibid.*, p. 209-10.

11. *Ibid.*, p. 210.

12. *Ibid.*, p. 209.

13. *Ibid.*, p. 71. Like so many German political theorists, Hess was addicted to the use of analogies. I think a comparison would show that in the first half of the century, political theorists most often took their analogies from the life cycles of plants, animals, and men, but that after 1850 it was more customary for them to find analogies in physics or chemistry. If this is true, perhaps the prestige lent by the alliance was decisive, and the change in allegiance might be taken as one more indication of the transition from romanticism to realism.

14. *Ibid.*, pp. 20-21.

15. *Ibid.*, p. 335.

16. *Ibid.*, p. 149.

17. *Ibid.*, p. 180.

18. Zlocisti, *op. cit.*, p. 22.

19. Hess, *Die Heilige Geschischte*, p. 339.

20. *Ibid.*, p. 165.

21. *Ibid.*, pp. 71-72.

22. *Ibid.*, p. 285.

23. *Ibid.*, pp. 279ff.

24. *Ibid.*, pp. 282-83.

25. *Ibid.*, pp. 248-49.

26. *Ibid.*, p. 333.

27. *Ibid.*, p. 330.

28. *Ibid.*, p. 345.

29. Moses Hess, *Die Europaeische Triarchie* (Leipzig, 1841), p. 157.
30. *Ibid.,* p. 167.

The True Socialist

1. Zlocisti, *op. cit.*, pp. 54ff. The fame of this paper is, of course, due to Marx's participation as editor. He began in October, 1842.
2. Hess, *Die Europaeische Triarchie*, p. 142.
3. *Ibid.*
4. Moses Hess, "Das Raetsel des 19. Jahrhunderts," *Rheinische Zeitung* (Beiblaetter 109-19), April, 1842; reprinted in Moses Hess, *Sozialistische Aufsaetze, 1841-1847,* ed., Theodore Zlocisti (Berlin, 1921), p. 12.
5. Moses Hess, "Deutschland und Frankreich in Bezug auf die Zentralisationsfrage," *Rheinische Zeitung* (Beiblatt 137), May 17, 1842; reprinted in Hess, *Sozialistische Aufsaetze,* p. 13.
6. *Ibid.*
7. Moses Hess, *Rheininsche Zeitung* (Beilblatt 177), June 26, 1842; reprinted in Hess, *Sozialistische Aufsaetze,* p. 24.
8. Moses Hess, "Religion und Sittlichkeit," *Rheinische Zeitung* (Beiblatt 216), August 4, 1842; reprinted in Hess, *Sozialistiche Aufsaetze,* pp.
9. Zlociti, *op. cit.*, pp. 110ff.
10. *Ibid.,* p. 113.
11. Moses Hess, "Ueber die Sozialistische Bewegung in Deutschland;" reprinted in Hess, *Sozialistische Aufsaetze,* p. 124.
12. *Ibid.,* p. 125.
13. Hess, *Die Europaeische Triarchie,* Foreword, unpaged.
14. Interestingly enough, Hess began his first systematic revision of Hegelianism into a philosophy of radical social reform just after he completed a thorough study of Fichte in 1840. Had Hess started with Fichte rather than Hegel he would hardly have found it necessary to insist upon the radicalism of German idealism. Fichte, of course, presented the most radical version of the development of the World-Spirit in history, and it was Fichte, not Hegel, who had the boldness to predict and describe the Utopia of the future. Nevertheless, Fichte was not as influential among the radicals of the *Vormaerz* as was Hegel— as the term *left-Hegelians* indicates. Correspondingly, when the left-Hegelians stressed the radical elements in Hegelianism, time and time again they said Hegel when they seemed to mean Fichte. Certainly this is true of Hess, although he never admitted his debt to the fiery orator of the Wars of Liberation. Partly, no doubt, this is to be explained by Hegel's popularity among those who led the seminars in philosophy at the German Universities during the late thirties and early forties—the

tendency was to attribute the dialectical method as applied to history mainly to Hegel, and little attention was paid to Fichte's historical writings. Then again, perhaps the left-Hegelians were put off by Fichte's Prussianism, or perhaps he was simply far too specific for their tastes. Hegel, of course, left the future manifestations of the Spirit undefined —one could provide one's own details. For the left-Hegelians were never united by a common goal, but by a common interpretation of the past. Consequently, when each began to fill in his own details, they came to a parting of the ways, and the movement was dissolved into a disparate group of ideologists: quietists, liberals, Christian-Democrats, Communists, Socialists, scientific Socialists and, with Hess, True Socialists.

15. August von Cieszkowski, *Prolegomena zur Historiosophie* (Berlin, 1838).
16. Moses Hess, "Die Gegenwaertige Krise der Deutschen Philosophie," reprinted in Hess, *Sozialistische Aufsaetze,* p. 9.
17. Hess, *Die Europaeische Triarchie,* p. 18.
18. *Ibid.,* Chap. One (Hess on Feuerbach).
19. *Ibid.,* p. 1.
20. *Ibid.,* p. 82.
21. *Ibid.,* p. 88.
22. Moses Hess, "Philosophie der Tat," *Ein und Zwanzig Bogen aus der Schweiz,* ed., George Herwegh, 1843; reprinted in Hess, *Sozialistische Aufsaetze. Ein und Zwanzig Bogen aus der Schweiz* was a collection of articles by German radicals. The title was meant to annoy the Prussian censors, for any book over twenty *Bogen* (a printer's measure) was free from censorship under Prussian law. Even under the tongue-in-cheek title of *Stunden der Andacht,* however, the book could not be smuggled into Germany, for the *Bund* had laws covering books of any size.
23. *Ibid.,* p. 37.
24. *Ibid.,* pp. 40ff.
25. *Ibid.,* p. 58.
26. There is, of course, still a great dispute raging as to the role played by ideas in dialectical materialism. I base my remarks mainly on Engels' discussion of dialectical materialism in his *Ludwig Feuerbach and the Outcome of Classical German Philosophy* (New York, 1941), especially Chap. IV; and his *Socialism, Utopian and Scientific* (New York, 1935), especially Chap. III.
27. Moses Hess, "Philosophie der Tat," *Sozialistische Aufsaetze,* p. 41.
28. Hess, *Die Europaeische Triarchie,* pp. 75-76.
29. Hess, "Philosophie der Tat," *Sozialistische Aufsaetze,* pp. 43ff.
30. *Ibid.,* p. 44.
31. Moses Hess, "Ueber die Not in unserer Gesellschaft und deren Abhilfe,"

Deutsches Buergerbuch (Darmstadt, 1845); and "Ueber das Geld-wesen," *Rheinische Jahrbuecher zur gesellschaftlichen Reform* (1845), I. Both are reprinted in Hess, *Sozialistische Aufsaetze.*

32. Hess, "Ueber das Geldwesen," *Sozialistische Aufsaetze,* p. 179.
33. *Ibid.,* p. 176.
34. Hess, "Ueber die Not," *Sozialistische Aufsaetze,* p. 138.
35. Max Stirner, *Der Einzige und Sein Eigenthum* (Leipzig, 1845); I have taken the quotation from Moses Hess, "Die Letzten Philosophen" (Darmstadt, 1845); reprinted in Hess, *Sozialistische Aufsaetze,* pp. 203-04.
36. *Ibid.,* p. 204.
37. Hess, "Ueber die Not," *Sozialistische Aufsaetze,* p. 161.
38. Hess, "Ueber das Geldwesen," *Sozialistische Aufsaetze,* p. 186.
39. *Ibid.,* p. 186.
40. Hess, "Ueber die Not," *Sozialistische Aufsaetze,* pp. 164ff.
41. Hess, "Ueber das Geldwesen," *Sozialistische Aufsaetze,* pp. 180-81.
42. Hess, "Ueber die Not," *Sozialistische Aufsaetze,* p. 151.
43. *Ibid.,* p. 156.
44. *Ibid.,* p. 142.
45. Moses Hess, "Kommunistische Bekenntnis in Fragen und Antworten," *Rheinische Jahrbuecher zur gesellschaftlichen Reform,* I, 1845; reprinted in Irma Goitein, *Probleme der Gesellschaft und des Staates bei Moses Hess* (Leipzig, 1931), p. 134.
46. Hess, "Ueber die Not," *Sozialistische Aufsaetze,* p. 161.

Between Utopianism and Scientism: Moses Hess, 1846-1875

1. Moses Hess, "Die Folgen der Revolution des Proletariats," *Deutsch-Bruesseler Zeitung,* 1847; reprinted in Hess, *Sozialistische Aufsaetze,* pp. 207-20.
2. Letter to Marx from Engels, Oct. 25, 26, 1847; in Marx/Engels, *Briefwechsel* (Berlin, 1949), I, 98.
3. Karl Marx, *Die Fruehschriften* (ed., Siegfried Landshut; Stuttgart, 1953), p. 226.
4. Letter to Engels from Marx, Mar. 17, 1845; in Marx/Engels, *Briefwechsel,* I, 21ff.
5. Letter to Marx from Engels, Nov. 19, 1844; in *ibid.,* I, 10.
6. Marx/Engels (and Hess!), *Die Deutsche Ideologie* (Berlin, 1953), p. 6. Hess wrote the section: "Der Dr. Georg Kuhlmann aus Holstein," pp. 575-87.
7. *Ibid.,* pp. 481-587. Also Engels, "Zwei Aufsaetze ueber die wahren Sozialisten," *Deutsche-Bruesseler Zeitung* (Summer, 1847).

8. Letter to Marx from Engels, Jan., 1845; in Marx/Engels, *Briefwechsel*, I, 14.

9. Helmut Hirsch, *Denker und Kaempfer* (Frankfurt a/M., 1955), pp. 99-110. See also footnote 10.

10. Letter to Marx from Engels, Feb. 22, 1845; in Marx/Engels, *Briefwechsel*, I, 19.

11. Zlocisti, *op. cit.*, p. 187.

12. Letter to Marx from Hess, May 29, 1846; in Hess/Marx, "Briefwechsel," *Der Kampf*, ed., J. P. Mayer, XXII (1929), 430.

13. *Ibid.*, p. 433.

14. Sidney Hook, *From Hegel to Marx* (New York, 1936). Permission to quote has been granted by *Humanities Press*, New York, New York.

15. As quoted in *ibid.*, p. 219.

16. Moses Hess, "Die Folgen der Revolution des Proletariats"; in *Sozialistische Aufsaetze*, pp. 207-30.

17. *Ibid.*, pp. 227-28.

18. *Ibid.*, p. 210.

19. *Ibid.*, p. 230.

20. *Ibid.*, pp. 209ff.

21. *Ibid.*, p. 215.

22. Letters to Herzen from Hess; in Goitein, *op. cit.*, pp. 166ff.

23. Letter to Herzen from Hess, March, 1850; reprinted in Goitein, *op. cit.*, p. 169.

24. Moses Hess, "Naturwissenschaften und Gesellschaftslehre," *Das Jahrhundert*, I, II (1856-57). (The article is scattered through both volumes.)

25. *Ibid.*, I, 171.

26. *Ibid.*, *passim.*

27. *Ibid.*, II, 288.

28. *Ibid.*, I, 290; II, 133.

29. Anonymous, "Offener Brief on Karl Marx," *Freiheit Arbeit*, XIII, Feb. 25, 1849, 3-4.

30. Zlocisti, *op. cit.*, Chap. Ten.

31. *Ibid.*, p. 252.

32. Moses Hess, "Jugement Dernier du vieux Monde Social," *Dokumente des Sozialismus* (Berlin, 1902), p. 540.

33. "Briefe Lassalles an Dr. [sic] Moses Hess," hrsg. Carl Gruenberg, *Archiv fuer die Geschichte des Sozialismus und der Arbeiterbewegung*, III (1913), 129-42.

34. As quoted in Zlocisti, *op. cit.*, p. 331.

35. As quoted in *ibid.*, p. 349.

36. Moses Hess, *Rechte der Arbeit* (Frankfurt a/M., 1863), pp. 17-18.

(Lecture given at Cologne and Duesseldorf for members of the Allgemeine Deutsche Arbeiterverein.)

37. *Ibid.*, p. 17.

38. *Ibid.*, pp. 18ff.

39. Ferdinand Lassalle, *Ueber Verfassungswesen* (Zuerich, 1863). See also Lassalle, *Zweiter Vortrag ueber Verfassungswesen* (Zuerich, 1863).

40. Hess, *Rechte der Arbeit*, passim.

41. *Ibid.*, p. 19.

42. *Ibid.*, p. 16. See also Maurice Hess, *La Haute Finance et L'Empire* (Paris, 1869), especially pp. 38ff.

43. See Hirsch, *op. cit.*, pp. 95ff. For further details about Hess's dealings with Napoleon III.

44. Hess, *Rechte der Arbeit*, p. 16.

45. *Ibid.*, p. 19.

46. *Ibid.*, p. 27.

47. Hess, *La Haute Finance*, p. 7.

48. Letter to Lassalle from Hess, Dec. 9, 1863; in *Ferdinand Lassalles Nachgelassene Briefe und Schriften*, hrsg. Gustav Mayer (Stuttgart und Berlin, 1925), V, 263-64.

49. Moses Hess, "Ferdinand Lassalle," *Journal des Actionnaires*, April, 1864.

50. Zlocisti, *op. cit.*, p. 406.

51. Moses Hess, *Une Nation déchue* (Bruxelles, 1871).

52. Moses Hess, *Dynamischer Stofflehre*, (Paris, 1877), I *(Komischer Teil)*, 5, 7.

53. *Ibid.*, p. 8.

Bibliography

For an excellent bibliography of Hess's works see the following publications of Edmund Silberner.

Silberner, Edmund. *Moses Hess; an annotated Bibliography.* New York: Burt Franklin, 1951.

————. "The works of Moses Hess." *Bulletin of the International Institute for Social History.* Numbers one and three, 1954.

I have listed only those works of Hess from which I have quoted or used for this study.

Books:

Hess, Moses. *Die Heilige Geschichte der Menschheit.* Stuttgart: Hallberger'sche Verlagshandlung, 1837.

————. *Die Europaeische Triarchie.* Leipzig: Wigand, 1841.

————. *Rom und Jerusalem.* Leipzig: Wengler, 1862.

————. *Dynamische Stofflehre. (Kosmischer Teil).* Paris: Verlag von Mme. Syb. M. Hess, Wittwe, 1877.

Articles: I have included only those which were useful for this study, and I have given complete references to the original publication only for those essays which are not included in:

Hess, Moses. *Sozialistische Aufsaetze, 1841-47.* Edited by Theodore Zlocisti, Berlin: Weltverlag, 1921.

————. "Was Wir Wollen." First published in Irma Goitein, *Probleme der Gesellschaft und des Staates bei Moses Hess,* Leipzig: Hirschfeld, 1931. (Contains also a criticism of Proudhon.)

———. "Kommunistisches Bekenntnis in Fragen und Antworten." In Goiten, *Probleme der Gesellschaft und des Staates bei Moses Hess.*

———. "Die Verhandlungen des gesetzgebenden Staatskoerpers der Republik Waadt ueber die Soziale Frage." *Rheinische Jahrbuecher zur gesellschaftlichen Reform,* II, 1846.

———. "Die Gesellschaftlichen Zustaende der civilisierten Welt (*Gesellschaftsspiegel* articles). Elberfeld und Iserlohn: Baedecker, 1846.

———. "Roter Katechismus fuer das Deutsche Volk." 1849/50. In Goiten, *Probleme der Gesellschaft und des Staates bei Moses Hess.*

———. "Jugement Dernier Du Vieux Monde Social." Partly translated into German by E. Bernstein in *Dokumente des Sozialismus.* Berlin: Verlag der Socialistischen Monatshefte, I, 1902.

———. "Naturwissenschaften und Gesellschaftslehre." *Das Jahrhundert,* I, II, 1856-57.

———. *Rechte der Arbeit.* (Pamphlet.) Frankfurt a/M.: R. Baist, 1863.

———. "La Haute Finance et l'Empire." Paris: Armand Le Chevelier, 1869.

———. "Die Soziale Revolution." *Volkstaat,* February, 1870.

———. "Une Nation déchue." Bruxelles: Bureau du peuple, 1871.

Marx, Engels, Hess. *Die Deutsche Ideologie.* Berlin: Dietz Verlag, 1953.

Secondary sources:

Cornu, Auguste. *Moses Hess et la gauche hégélienne.* Paris: Libraire Felix Alcan, 1934.

Goitein, Irma. *Probleme der Gesellschaft und des Staates bei Moses Hess.* Leipzig: Hirschfeld, 1931.

Groethuysen, B. "Les jeunes hégéliens et les origines du socialisme contemporain en Allemagne." *Revue Philosophique,* VC, 1923.

Hammacher, Emil. "Zur Wuerdigung des 'wahren' Sozialismus." *Archv fuer die Geschichte des Sozialismus und der Arbeiterbewegung,* I, 1911.

Hirsch, Helmut. *Denker und Kaempfer.* Frankfurt a/M.: Europaeische Verlagsanstalt, 1955.

Hook, Sidney. "Karl Marx and Moses Hess." *New International,* I, 1934.

———. *From Hegel to Marx.* New York: Reynal, 1936.

Lukács, Georg. "Moses Hess und die Probleme der idealistischen Dialektik." *Archiv fuer die Geschichte des Sozialismus und der Arbeiterbewegung,* XII, 1926.

Mielcke, Karl. *Deutscher Fruehsozialismus.* (Weitling and Hess.) Stuttgart: Cotta, 1931.

Silberner, Edmund. "Moses Hess." *Historia Judaica,* XIII, Part One, April, 1951.

Singer, Hannah. *Die Theorie des Wahren Sozialismus.* (Dissertation.) Quakenbrueck: Trute, 1930.

Zlocisti, Theodor. *Moses Hess, Der Vorkaempfer des Sozialismus und Zionismus.* Zweite vollkommen neu bearbeitete Auflage. Berlin: Weltverlag, 1921.

The following were published after my research was completed. However, they are far too important to go unnoticed.

Edmund Silberner, *Moses Hess Briefwechsel,* 'S-Gravenhage: Mouton & Co., 1959.

————. *The Works of Moses Hess,* Leiden: E. J. Brill, 1958.

————."Der junge Moses Hess im Lichte bisher unerforschter Quellen," *International Review of Social History,* Bd. III, 1958, pp. 43-70, 239-68.

Index

Edited by Bernard Harris
Cover designed by S. R. Tenenbaum
Set in Linotype Caledonia and Venus
Printed on Warren English Finish paper
and Sorg Plate Finished cover
Manufactured in the United States of America

MCO NO. 294